How to Get in Football Shape

STRENGTH TRAINING

Front cover image provided by Comstock Images.
Back cover photography and all black and white photography,
excluding DVD grabs, provided by Keith Hadley.

Frisbee® is a registered trademark of the Whammo Corporation.
SwimEx® is a registered trademark of the SwimEx Corporation.
Hand strength information compiled with reference to *Mastery of Hand Strength*,
by John Brookfield, published by Ironmind Enterprises, 1995.

Published by Cool Springs Press, a Division of Thomas Nelson, Inc.,
P.O. Box 141000, Nashville, Tennessee, 37214

Library of Congress Cataloging-in-Publication Data is available.
ISBN 1-591860-05-9

First printing 2003
Printed in the United States of America
10 9 8 7 6 5 4 3 2 1

Editor: Ramona D. Wilkes
Copyeditor: Jason Zasky
Proofing: Sally Graham
Production/Design: Joey McNair of Defy Creative

Visit the Thomas Nelson website at www.ThomasNelson.com

The National Football League Coaches Association Presents

How to Get in Football Shape

STRENGTH TRAINING

FOR BOYS 14 AND OLDER

BERT HILL

Nashville, Tennessee
A Division of Thomas Nelson, Inc.
www.ThomasNelson.com

Contents

Foreword vi

Introduction vii

Chapter One
A Primer 1

Chapter Two
Getting Started 11

Chapter Three
The Weight Room 21

Chapter Four
Weight Training 49

Chapter Five
General Exercises 53

Chapter Six
Specialized Programs 77

The Six Week Program 87

Percentage Guide 125

Strength Training Journal 129

DVD Index 135

About Bert Hill 136

Foreword

On behalf of the National Football League Coaches Association (NFLCA), I am proud to present this book to young athletes across America. It's one of many projects undertaken by the NFLCA that provide tomorrow's high school and college players with proven fundamentals that work on the field and off, in the classroom and at home.

The NFLCA was founded in 1996 primarily to assist retired NFL coaches with issues such as salaries, insurance, pensions, and other benefits. But the educational and instructional aspect of our work has blossomed in recent years. To date, we have published three instructional books for youths. Our coaches participate in many clinics for junior level, high school, and college coaches. We have produced three highly regarded instructional videotapes, and we are now examining other ways to share NFL coaches' insights with youth, high school, and college coaches around the country.

These tools are just the early fruits of the NFLCA's commitment to educating young football players, their parents, and their coaches. As coaches, we know that from quality instruction comes quality play. From quality play comes enjoyment, self-worth, and confidence. We see it in the eyes of the young men we coach every day. With this and the increasingly broad line of NFLCA products and services now available, we're certain that we'll being seeing that look in the eyes of more happily determined kids for years to come.

Larry Kennan
Executive Director
National Football League Coaches Association
Washington, DC

Introduction

In my career in strength training I have had the pleasure of working with some of the finest athletes in the world. For instance, during my time with the Detroit Lions I worked very closely with a young man whom I believe will be remembered as one of the greatest football players of all time: Barry Sanders.

As you might guess, it's enormously gratifying to feel as though you might have had a positive impact on a guy like Barry. But Barry, through his own skill, his early coaching, and his standout strength training at Oklahoma State, was well on his way to greatness before I ever met him. That's the case with most NFL players. They have already become strong, powerful, coordinated athletes. As an NFL strength coach, my job is to take them to the next level. While that's exciting and challenging work, I've often wished there were a way that I could reach multitudes of young athletes early on and help them build a solid foundation of strength training. That's what this book is intended to do: Give young football players a starting point and a plan for developing real football strength.

I want to applaud the National Football League Coaches Association for undertaking this project. I have no doubt that the young athletes who study this book and the other books in the NFLCA series will grow in strength and athleticism and ultimately enjoy football even more. In the end, that's what the sport is all about.

Good Luck.

Bert Hill
Dallas, TX

ChapterOne
A Primer

I f you've pulled this book off the shelf, it means you're serious or at least curious about getting into "football shape." As the title states, this book deals with strength training. Strength training is often confused with working out, but they are dissimilar activities, and it's important to appreciate the differences early on.

▲ An increase in muscle mass is only one of the many beneficial results of a strength training program.

Working out is an end in itself. You do it to relieve stress or accomplish something short-term. It's incidental. For instance, you may just want to break a sweat or work off a heavy meal. You can work out two or three times and never come back to it, and it's still a workout. On the other hand, training is a dedicated, organized approach toward reaching a long-term goal. When we talk about training for football, we're talking about assessing where we are, deciding where we need to be, determining the best way to achieve that goal, and then actually executing the plan.

The purpose of this book is to help youngsters (ages fourteen and older) learn the value of strength training and to give them programs they can use over time to increase the specific strengths that football requires. The ultimate goal is not simply to increase strength, it's to increase *football strength* as a means toward enhancing overall on-the-field performance. We're not training to be weight lifters here. Sure, I may show you exercises that come from other disciplines or other sports, but I only do so because they have a very high carryover value to football performance.

The goal of your training should not be to maximize how much weight you can lift. The goal is perfect technique with the right amount of weight. That not only makes it strength training, but it assures us that the work will carry over into football technique.

The Benefits of Strength Training

There are four football-related benefits to a properly supervised strength training program:

1. Increase in lean muscle mass
2. Improved flexibility
3. Improved reaction time
4. Increase in the ability to produce power

▲ Strength training is a proven, vital contributor to on-the-field success.

Notice we talk about *power* in the above list, not strength. Why is there no reference to strength? Well, strength, by definition, is "Force x Distance." There is no speed element in pure strength. If I load a table up with 10,000 pounds and it takes me eight hours to push it across the room you would say I'm a strong man. But in football, power is more important than strength because power implies speed. In fact, the formula for power is "Force x Distance divided by Time." So if you wanted to know not just how strong I was, but how powerful I was, then you would put a time frame on how long it takes me to push that table across the room. The faster I can push it, the more powerful I am.

In football, speed and power are everything. That's true for every level—elementary, junior high, high school, college, and professional. So what we do in our training program is to develop strength that can actually be demonstrated as power.

Oddly, the foundation of a thoughtful strength training program for football is not really strength, it's technique. Early on you should work conscientiously to refine and perfect your technique. Then, as your technique improves, add a little bit of

> *In football, speed and power are everything.*

weight, which is going to improve your strength. Once you have a base level of technique and strength, then you can start incorporating exercises at a faster pace—in other words, moving the bar quicker, moving the bar faster—ultimately creating power. That's how you tie it all together. **Technique leads to strength, strength leads to power, and power improves on-the-field performance.**

How critical is proper technique? I recently had the opportunity to work with defensive end Luther Ellis, who is currently playing for the Detroit Lions. Overall, Luther is probably the strongest player I've ever coached. He's a legitimate 550-pound bench presser. I don't know how much he can squat, because I've never let him do more than 600 pounds. In addition, he can power clean upwards of 350 to 400 pounds. We have some heavy dumbbells in our weight room that go up to 170 pounds, and I've had several guys that have lifted 130s, 140s, or even 150s. Luther decided one day he was going to do the 170s. So we rolled them over and put those big dumbbells on top of him, and he pressed them up three times. He's the only man I can remember who could do that many repetitions with the 170s.

I've seen several people attempt it, but 170 pounds in each hand—it's a feat just to balance that weight, much less press it.

Even with all that strength, Luther will tell you this: If he gets away from his football technique—keeping his knees bent and staying in a position of superior leverage—he can go up against an offensive lineman who has nowhere near his strength and lose. Even with his incredible strength he needs to use proper technique. So regardless of how much strength you have, if it's not applied with correct technique, it's useless.

Good weight training is highly personalized. You need to know your own strengths and weaknesses, where you are and where you hope to be. You need to take an organized approach, and you need specific goals. For a serious young football player to get the latest copy of a muscle magazine, tear out a workout, and go do it once or twice won't cut it.

> *. . . regardless of how much strength you have, if it's not applied with correct technique, it's useless.*

Plus, weight training is only part of the picture. It's one of many things you need to do if you are going to be a successful athlete. There are guys who can lift a lot of weight and have great power, but they can't play football. Football itself requires specific talents (physical and mental) that you have to practice and master. Strength training is going to help you stay injury free, which is a critical factor for success during the season. That should be your number one goal. Secondly, you want to become more powerful. Whether it's your feet or your hands—whatever tools that you use to be a successful football player—that's what you've got to work on.

In our society, from the time a boy can walk he gets plenty of encouragement to be strong and athletic. It's not surprising that some boys want to begin weight training programs at age six or seven. From the experiences

I've had—and I've had the opportunity to visit with a lot of different peo-ple in different disciplines, medical as well as athletic—it's best to wait until you are "post-pubescent." In other words, you're not ready for real weight training until you've grown some body hair. That tells you that you're at least halfway through puberty and your bones and muscles can handle the load. The biggest problem with starting weight training too early is that the bones have not fully developed. There is significant risk in being pre-pubescent and lifting weights.

How and when to start training depends upon the individual and the exercises in question. As a rule of thumb, I wouldn't do any heavy leg training (such as squats) until you're fourteen or fifteen years old. That doesn't mean you have to be idle until then. One very interesting finding about youth weight training has come out of Eastern Europe. Back in the days of the Cold War, the Soviet Union and East Germany were known to start training kids at four or five years old. These kids didn't lift

> **You can do a lot of weight-type training without actually using weights.**

heavy weights, but they practiced technique with things like broom handles for bars and bicycle tires for weights. By the time they were old enough to handle actual weights, their technique was flawless and their ligaments were meticulously prepared for the kind of stress that strength training would eventually place on them.

I think there is a lot of value in simulated weight work. I also believe that sit-ups, push-ups, chin-ups, running, and other playful activities can improve strength. You can do a lot of weight-type training without actually using weights. Years ago, when small farms were more prevalent, guys would come off the farm strong as oxen. They'd never lifted a weight in their lives, but they worked hard all day. I wouldn't recommend practicing a formalized weight-training regimen until you are fourteen or fifteen years old. But until

▲ Body weight exercises such as sit-ups or push-ups can serve as a good foundation for athletes who are too young for a serious weight-based strength training program.

then—say, if you're ten or eleven and playing Pop Warner ball—I would recommend a marine-style program (chin-ups, dips, sit-ups, abdominal work, stepping over logs, etc). This is movement-based physical training that doesn't require weights. In exercises such as these you're still doing weight training, it's just that you're using your own body weight.

For a ten-year-old, I would recommend body weight exercises two or three days a week for a period of six or seven weeks. Then start working in a couple of weight training exercises just focusing on technique. If you can do twelve to fifteen repetitions of an exercise, you might add a pound to each side of the bar. (There are companies that make half-pound and quarter-pound weights so you can add to the barbell in smaller increments.) I would develop four or five exercises. Try to make your workout a total body workout so you're not focusing only on arm development or legs or another isolated area.

A lot of kids and parents shy away from strength training due to fear of injury. The fear is there for a reason. You *can* get hurt lifting weights. I've seen guys drop barbells on their toes and even on their chests. I think you overcome the fear by emphasizing technique and by emphasizing the fact that you don't have to lift a tremendously heavy amount of weight to get a benefit. You're training for one reason—to improve your football ability. You'll incur enough injuries out on the field actually playing the game. You can't afford to sustain one while you're preparing. Safety is mostly just paying attention to detail and understanding that you're smarter than the weights. I've had players who did a 400-pound squat with four plates on each side of the barbell. They racked the bar, and then when they went to unload the bar they took all four plates off one side. Inevitably, the bar tipped and hit the floor. I had to remind them not to let the weights outsmart them.

I strongly encourage proper spotting technique. I teach players the proper way to spot somebody so that the lifter is always in a position of safety. There's always somebody there or there's a piece of equipment there to keep injury from occurring. I would not allow anybody under fifteen years old to train unsupervised. There should be somebody around to help if you get caught in a bad situation.

The Key Safety Rules Are:

- Always use proper lifting technique.
- Check the environment around you. Make sure that it is set up to accommodate whatever activity you're performing.

◀ Just like football, strength training is a team sport. I strongly encourage athletes to use spotters.

Also, I think that strength training and football need to be kept in perspective. It's important that you have a lot of other things going on in your life beyond football and weight training. I encourage you to get involved in a variety of activities and to participate in other sports. This affords you the opportunity to get out and do movement skills in other sports—soccer, basketball, baseball, softball—whatever it might be. You'd be amazed at how many of the skills required in other sports can eventually help prepare for football.

I can think of another important factor that needs to be discussed here. A man named Daniel Goleman recently wrote a book called *Emotional Intelligence* (Bantam Books, October 1995). He said the most important thing that parents can teach their children is what he referred to as "self-imposed delay of gratification." What that means is that you need to sacrifice today for something you may want tomorrow. Here's an example: Researchers once did a study where they brought kids in who were three- to five-years-old, and this guy sat them down one at a time and said, "OK, here's a piece of candy. Now, I've got an errand that I've got to run. I'll be back in two minutes. You can have that piece of candy while I'm gone, or if you can wait until I come back before you eat it, I'll give you two more pieces to go with it." Then he'd leave the room. Of course, the kids that couldn't wait grabbed the candy and ate it right away, but some kids found a way to distract themselves. They were rewarded with three pieces. The researchers then looked at these kids twelve to fifteen years down the road and found that those who delayed gratification were far more successful in school and in sports than the kids who didn't.

That is the same thing we're looking for here. You may not be as strong a football player as you'd like to be, but if you get a plan and commit to executing your plan every day, then you will eventually achieve that goal.

Pain and Gain:
Can You Have One without the Other?

The 1970s gave rise to a saying that has bugged me since I first heard it:

"No pain, no gain." I don't know what to say about that phrase other than it's dangerously misguided. The suggestion is that you cannot make a significant improvement in weight training without experiencing pain. I'm not saying it's easy to get up at 6:00 in the morning to get your workout in; if that's pain so be it. But if we're talking about actual physical, bodily pain, you want to avoid that.

At times, I have done some painful training with advanced athletes—particularly with professional players—when we're trying to get through mental sticking points. But at no time do I ever take or recommend that approach with young football players, whether they're elementary, junior high, or high school guys. That's just not part of our program.

ChapterTwo
Getting Started

I think the best way to get started is to stick with basic exercises—*multi-joint* exercises that train the entire body. Generally speaking these are exercises that involve several muscle groups crossing over several joints. For example, a *single-joint* exercise would be a line triceps press where you're lying down on a bench, your elbow is in a

▲ **The bench press is a classic multi-joint exercise.**

fixed position, and you are lowering and extending the weight, but the only movement is occurring at the elbow. An example of a multi-joint exercise could be a bench press where there's movement at the wrist, the elbow, and the shoulder as you lower the weight to the chest and press it to arms' length. A barbell squat is another great example of a multi-joint exercise. With the barbell on your back, you bend at the knee so that the ankles, the knees, and the hips are all involved in the exercise. The multi-joint exercises are safer because they distribute the force or the load over several joints and don't isolate one particular muscle group or joint. It's especially important for you to use multi-joint exercises because you'll get an overall training effect and not put too much focus on any one particular muscle group.

Form

▲ **Be a stickler for proper technique.**

That leads us into developing correct form. I'm a visual person, but some people are aural—that is, they understand things best when they hear them. For me a picture is worth a thousand words. If you can show me the correct form either by doing the exercise, showing me a video, or opening a book, I can generally take that information in and repeat it. Some people do well just by being told what to do. But ultimately good technique is only going to come through repetition—that is, practicing over and over and over. It's extremely valuable to have somebody there who can make the corrections if you're not using the right technique and get you to where you can actually feel the difference between good technique and bad technique. Technique in weight lifting at some point has to be like technique in a sport. You can't think about it. You just do it, and your body puts you in the right position.

That said, form and technique in any activity can be over-coached. You see it when a young football player who has only *studied* defenses, *studied* form, and *studied* technique finally gets into a game. He has to think about and process everything that's going on around him before he can execute. He's so caught up in analyzing what's happening as each play unfolds that he ends up doing nothing. We call it "paralysis by analysis."

In Detroit, I had the opportunity to work with ex-Lions running back Barry Sanders, a guy who is always going to be listed as one of the all-time great football players (and in my mind, he's also one of the world's all-time great people). You'd think that in order to achieve his remarkable skill level, his training regimen would have to be very complex. Wrong. His entire program basically consisted of three lifts: a bench press, a hang clean, and a squat. In a *hang clean*, you pick the bar up off the floor and start it just above or just below your knee. Then, in one movement, you carry it to the shoulders. Barry felt that his success in professional football could be attributed to his college strength coach, John Stucky. Barry was only recruited by a handful of colleges. He was 5'5" coming out of high school—of course he'll tell you he was 5'7" or 5'9"—and weighed about 165 pounds. He ended up attending Oklahoma State and coach Stucky had Barry do hang cleans and squats. Barry felt that working his legs so hard was the key to his success. That's what enabled him to make the unbelievable moves he made—those unforgettable cuts and darts.

> *. . . not everyone takes easily to weight training.*

Of course, not everyone takes easily to weight training. Often a youngster might be a pretty good athlete and he might take pride in that, but he knows he's not very strong. He gets embarrassed when some guy that he can beat like a drum in one-on-one drills proves to be stronger than he is in the weight room. From time to time I have taken guys, pulled them aside when nobody else is around, and worked with them one-on-one. You'd be surprised at the change in attitude. They quickly get caught up with the rest of the group without suffering any embarrassment. That has generally been a pretty effective approach.

Results vs. Expectations

How do you measure results when you are just getting into weight training? I can work with a youngster, see what his technique looks like, see how much he weighs and how much weight he's lifting. Then I can sit down with him after I've seen those factors, and if I can get him to work on a regular basis then maybe I can get him to gain two or three pounds of lean body weight over the course of eight weeks. By that point in time I would expect him to press a certain amount of weight.

What should your goal be? What's reasonable for you to attain? Controlling expectations is a big part of successful strength training. That's where lots of people run into problems when they first start in a training program. I've seen kids who expect their squats or bench press totals to increase 50 pounds in five weeks. That's very unlikely. An increase of 1 or 2 pounds a week is more like it. You need to have a realistic understanding that it takes time.

Ultimately, results are shaped by several different forces. As a coach, I'm always monitoring these four factors:

1. Is your technique sound? Is there something you can do to increase the amount of weight you can lift simply by improving your technique?

▲ Technique is one of four key factors that will determine your strength training success.

2. What is your body weight/body fat and what should it be considering the position you play? Is it important for you to gain 5 pounds if you're a wide receiver or defensive back? Is that going to slow you down or speed you up? (Actually, if you put on lean body weight you're usually going to get faster.) I have to make sure that when I'm putting weight on you, I'm not just putting weight on for the scales, but that I'm putting weight on that's going to be functional.

3. How long are you going to be training? Each youngster's availability is going to be different.

4. The last one is obvious: Hard work. When you're truly working hard, you're totally focused, pouring everything you have into what you're doing at that moment. How do you get to that level of focus? To me, you get there by coming into the weight room with a focused goal in mind of what you're going to get accomplished that day. I like for my athletes to know ahead of time—before they get into the weight room—what their workout is going to consist of and what they feel they're going to be able to lift that day. Then you focus on that.

▲ **Ultimately, your desire, your willingness to work hard, will determine your success.**

When you come in and as you're going through your warm-up sets, you're preparing yourself mentally and physically for your last few sets and your top weight for the day. You're not talking about the weather or what you did on vacation or what you're going to do next weekend. You're focused on what's going on with your workout and your training. To me, that's what hard work is all about.

That level of focus and hard work is not easy to achieve, especially in today's world which is so full of distractions. When I was working with the Detroit Lions under head coach Bobby Ross, one of our assistant coaches had a nephew who was going to play college football in the fall. This assistant wanted the boy to come to training camp with us and work as an intern. The boy's parents were divorced, and he really didn't have a lot of guidance or a father figure in his life. The Lions gave him a job with the equipment guys. It didn't work out too well. He was on the phone all night to his girlfriend, and then he'd be in a daze all day, sometimes actually dozing off during work. Eventually the equipment guys got fed up and wanted to run him out of camp. I said, "Send him down here and I'll let him help me in the weight room." Then I told him, "Here's the deal. You can either go home or you can come down here and work with me. If you work with me, we're working out twice a day." I said, "I'm preparing for an NFL season and you've got college football to prepare for, so we're going to be busy. We're going to work out at 6:00 in the morning and 9:00 at night. If you're late or if you miss a single workout, you can just pack up your stuff and go."

He said, "OK." Well, initially this kid wanted to talk about everything—

> **You can't necessarily develop somebody's confidence and commitment overnight . . .**

what was going on at camp, this, that, and the other thing. I finally told him, "There is no talking. If we can't talk about something related to what you're doing in your workout then we don't talk." It was interesting to see him go from somebody who was totally unfocused to a guy who suddenly had a mission. I bring this example up because very often focus and determination have to be learned. It's not innate in everybody. You can't necessarily develop somebody's confidence and commitment overnight, but once you have developed it, that's when you can take an athlete to the next level.

Some of the most focused guys I've ever worked with were Chris Spielman (a great linebacker out of Ohio State University), Marc Spindler (a defensive lineman from the University of Pittsburgh), and Danny Owens (a defensive lineman from the University of Southern California). These guys didn't want to lift with the

> **. . . often focus and determination have to be learned. It's not innate in everybody.**

crowd. They had very clear and very different expectations and goals in mind. They would come in at about 6:30 in the morning during the off-season so that they could train together and work for the specific goal they had in mind each and every day. I think they taught me more than I ever taught them about the concept of training and camaraderie.

Every workout became a not-so-subtle competition, whether it was who did the most repetitions, or who could lift the most weight, or who had the best time when we were running drills. They had an interesting competition one day in the training room. We had just gotten in this new device called a SwimEx®. It's just like a swimming pool, but an internal pump makes the water rush at you so you can actually swim in place—almost like a treadmill for swimmers. They competed to find out who could stay under water for the longest period of time while directly facing this pump that was pushing water out at about twenty miles per hour. I don't know if he won or not, but Spindler ended up going to the hospital because the chlorine and the pressure of the water on his eyeballs created a problem severe enough that he had to get his eyes washed out. That's a bad example because the contest was a little foolish, but it shows how aggressively focused they were on being the best in every single facet of conditioning and endurance.

Everybody is motivated by something. It's always interesting to watch the evolution of NFL players. When they come in as rookies, they've only had praise for most of their lives. Then on top of that, they now have more money than they've ever had in their lives. As a result, they often lose focus early on. Usually, by their third year they realize that they're human and there are people better at the position than they are. Also, they come to the realization that they're not going to be alive, much less a star, for the rest of eternity. It's at this point when something clicks and their attitude almost inevitably begins to change.

> *I encourage you to develop good role models. Find and bond with guys who have focus, drive, and determination.*

That's why early training is so important to overcoming the distractions and temptations of the modern world. For better or worse, the strongest influence in many of your lives is peer pressure. If you don't associate with the right peers, there's no telling where you're headed. I encourage you to develop good role models. Find and bond with guys who have focus, drive, and determination. They may not always be the "coolest" kids. I didn't necessarily "fit in" when I was growing up. Then again, I didn't really care. That kind of independent thinking should be part of your mental preparation.

Keep It Simple

When it comes time to designing a program, does one size fit all or should the program adapt to the individual? I think when we're talking about the junior high, high school, and college athlete, a general overall program is all that's really needed. A teenager doesn't require a whole lot of specialization. I would recommend that you keep it simple, doing multi-joint exercises that allow you to use the most amount of weight. Specialization and adaptation will come as you get older, and even then it should be based on emerging strengths and weaknesses and the injuries you've had. In football, you're liable to

> **Specialization and adaptation will come as you get older . . .**

get nicked up so you do have to adapt your training program to try to keep as strong and as healthy as possible, all the while working around injuries. If you have a lack of flexibility in a certain area then you have to adapt the exercises you're doing while you're trying to improve flexibility in that particular area. As you get older you can get further into individualization.

When I was with the Detroit Lions, I had the opportunity to work with an offensive lineman named Mike Utley. Mike and I hit it off real well, and I thoroughly respected his work ethic. He was extremely strong in the legs and could squat over 650 pounds. Mike was not real strong in his upper body, but he could run like a gazelle. He would score A-pluses on any running test you put him through and was always in great shape. What I tried to do with him was to maintain his leg strength and focus a little bit more on developing upper body strength. That's an example of customizing a program based on personal history.

Be Positive

You may be familiar with Mike's story. In 1991, we were playing the Los Angeles Rams at the Silverdome in Pontiac, Michigan. We had the ball down on the Rams' 17-yard line. It was a pass play, and Mike dropped back to block Tracy Rocker of the Rams. The ball was thrown, and we scored a touchdown. But as Mike went to block Tracy, he got pulled down into a pile, and while no one immediately realized the extent of the injury, Mike suffered spinal cord damage. He was paralyzed from the waist down.

When the doctors and trainers carried Mike off the field, he gave everybody that famed "thumbs up" sign as they wheeled him into the tunnel. This happened over eleven years ago, and Mike is still determined to walk again. It's his courage in facing this problem and his work ethic that brought that football team together. That year we ended up playing in the NFC Championship game against the Washington Redskins for an opportunity to go to the Super Bowl, and it was largely due to the inspiration Mike gave us. Interestingly enough, since the injury, Mike has continued with weight training. As I mentioned before, when he and I started working together the goal was to make him stronger in the upper body, and he certainly is stronger right now. He can press more now than he did prior to the injury.

Of course, attitude is so important. One of my favorite quotes was first conveyed to me by coach Bobby Ross when he first took over the head coaching job in Detroit. It's from the poem *Attitude* by Charles Swindoll. In the poem, Swindoll says, "I am convinced that life is ten percent what happens to me and ninety percent how I react to it." In the case of Mike Utley, it's completely true. If you take that attitude into whatever you're trying to accomplish, you're going to be set up for success.

ChapterThree

The Weight Room

The weight room can be a dangerous place. Whenever I work with high school players I have an orientation program in which I demonstrate every exercise with an unloaded barbell. Then I let them do the exercise, making sure that they understand how I want them to breathe, where I want them to grip the barbell, and precisely how I

▲ **A weight room can be an intimidating and dangerous place.**

want the exercise done. I take them through each exercise, give them all the coaching points about safety and spotting technique, and then have them work with each other on technique and spotting with an unloaded barbell. This way I make sure everything is being done correctly before starting the program.

The weight room can also be an intimidating place. Of course, you need to know that you're not expected to lift everything all at once. Coaches should be there to guide and teach you. I've found that once a young athlete understands that I have a system in place that's going to help him to achieve his goals, he gets over that initial intimidation.

Now, not all bodies are created equal. One of the hardest parts of managing a group workout is making a youngster who can only bench press 100 pounds feel comfortable working out next to a guy who can do twice that. I recommend grouping yourselves together according to strength, but even in a group setting, strength training is an individual journey—an individual battle to develop and improve.

> ## If you're training for a sport, then the sport activity is the primary focus.

The first thing I look at when I start an athlete out on a strength program is time. How much time are you willing or able to commit? Suppose you have a total per-session time of sixty to ninety minutes. I would divide that time block into segments—allotting a certain amount of time for warm-up, flexibility, speed, agility, and of course, weights.

The exercises are then determined based on how much time you have. I've ranked them based on what I think are the most productive exercises that could help a particular individual. If you have thirty minutes you should factor how many sets you're going to do, how many repetitions, and how much rest time. How much rest time you are doing between sets is really going to be your determining factor. You come up with X number of minutes. Then it boils itself down to probably three to five exercises. Again, we're specifying multi-joint, total-body type exercises.

Before we get too far along we need to determine the goal of your program. What are you trying to accomplish? If you're training for a sport, then the sport activity is the primary focus. Focus on trying to improve football performance. The next thing you've got to look at is the time span of the entire program, measured from the beginning of the program until the day of competition. Look at training for a sport in multiple phases. You have an off-season program. You have a program that you want to try to get accomplished during your training camp. Then you're going to shift to an in-season mode, and once the season comes to a close you may have play-offs that might require a slightly different approach. Once the season is over, you should have a short period of what I call "active rest."

I measure where a newcomer is and how he's progressing by the amount of weight he can lift or the number of repetitions he can do and the relationship of those amounts to his body weight. You can set short-term and long-term goals based on those numbers.

I need a minimum of six weeks to get a player to show improvement in a strength training program. That may seem like a long time, but you need to account for a break-in period and then allow a little time at the end for that extra push to get to the level of desired improvement. When starting weight training, you need to remember that you need at least six weeks of uninterrupted training in order to see real results.

Motivation

At this point we need to differentiate between goals and expectations. To me, the goal is something the athlete has in mind, and the expectation is what the coach is aiming for. When dealing with a first-time guy, you're going to see improvement in a very short period of time because it's all potential. If you've never done any strength work there's only an upside. As long as you set realistic, obtainable goals and

▲ Have the correct motivation. If you're entering a football strength training program in hopes of looking like a body builder, you're making a mistake.

put them in time frames, you'll be fine. Then the only issue—and it's a big one—is *motivation*.

What's motivating you to want to do this, and what keeps you going day after day? The answer should be success. Certainly the overall goal is enhanced on-the-field performance. But since that won't be evident for a few weeks you also need to set some short-term goals. Set them on a weekly basis or a monthly basis if you're in a longer-term program, and make them very realistic. As athletes see success, their motivation increases. If it's a group, everyone needs to understand that they're not all necessarily going to increase at the same rate. You'll see guys whose leg strength starts taking off while their upper body development stagnates. Then they start getting stronger in the upper body and their legs will stagnate. The body is a funny mechanism, but if you keep working it, you're going to reach your full potential.

> **What's motivating you to want to do this, and what keeps you going day after day? The answer should be success.**

Some of you may be motivated more by improved physical appearance than by enhanced on-the-field performance. Your final appearance is going to be based on the type of training that you do, but you need to keep in mind that the whole purpose of this training is to become a better player. An interesting example is middle linebacker Brian Urlacher of the Chicago Bears. When you see Brian on the field he's not this huge, barrel-chested intimidating guy. The key to his success is his speed, quickness, and athletic ability. His legs and lower body have been specifically developed to enable him to play the game at a very high level. Remember that football is played on your feet, and even though you are going to see some players with big upper bodies, it's even more important that they have powerful legs and great agility.

In other words, it's a mistake to enter a football strength training regimen in the hope that you'll come out looking like Arnold Schwarzenegger. Arnold's strength training was designed specifically to make him a world-class body builder. Those same exercises would interfere with a football player's development. Football players don't necessarily need huge, well-defined muscles. Football requires speed, quickness, guts, and mobility. I don't care how strong or how big you are, you're not going to play this game unless you can move, hit, and be hit. There's documented evidence of guys who could bench press the whole weight room but weren't good football players because they didn't have the other key assets. I think that getting a huge upper body may be a by-product of football strength training, but I don't think that should be the goal in itself.

DVD Review

At any level, abdominal strength is vital to effective, injury-free football. Here NFL star Johnny Morton displays his "ab" strength.

Focus: Trunk and Lower Body

The trunk (your abdominal muscles and lower back) and lower body are my particular focus in this section. They are key to football success. Why? In a game of football—say, in executing a tackle—you're going to make contact with your shoulders. That force is directed from the legs and the hips up and through the shoulders. The trunk is right between the legs and the shoulders, so it acts almost like a shock absorber. When a player with a weak trunk hits somebody with his shoulder pads, the softest area is always going to give first, and his midsection will roll up like an accordion. Not only will the tackle be ineffective, but that shock to the tackler's midsection can cause serious injuries. On the other hand, when a guy who has a well-developed trunk and lower back makes a tackle, all the force from his legs and shoulders is delivered directly to his opponent. He'll make a more effective tackle, and he'll greatly reduce his own risk of injury. So it's very important in the game of football to develop your trunk and lower body.

These days, "dinosaur training" is a buzzword in the weight training world. Dinosaurs are defined as guys training with the same methods that people used in the 1920s, 30s, and 40s prior to the discovery of modern techniques. Back then, a guy who was developing his trunk picked up heavy sand bags or logs and carried those around. They actually did functional movements. I think you can mimic some of those when you're working the trunk. Pick up some dumbbells and carry them overhead, or hold a weight plate while doing some twisting motions. The old-fashioned bent press is an exercise that's been forgotten by most people. In it, you take a weight (and I would want you to start with something light) and hold it at your shoulder. Then press your body under the bar or the dumbbell and stand up. This exercise requires you to turn and twist and put yourself and your trunk in multi-dimensional situations with some resistance. That makes sense because when you're on a football field, the activity does not take place on a single plane. Football is multi-dimensional—you're turning, you're twisting, you're hitting, and you're absorbing hits.

A simple way to develop the lower back is to do what we call a *hyperextension*. Lie on the floor on your stomach. Have a friend hold your ankles while you put your hands behind your head. Then raise your shoulders or your chest up off the floor, hold it for a half a count and then go back down. It's the simplest way to develop your lower back muscles and keep your trunk strong.

▲ A hyperextension is a simple way to develop the lower back.

From that we go to variations: Raise up and turn one shoulder back and to the right side and then come back down. Raise up, this time turn back and to the left. Then down. So you also train the lower back in a turning, multi-dimensional type of program. If you're training your lower abdominal the way we just discussed where you're picking up a sand bag, you could put it on your right shoulder and make a half turn to the right and come back and set it on the floor. Then pick it up and put it on your left shoulder and make a

half turn and come back and set it on the floor. Pick it up and walk with it for 10-15 paces. Then throw it in the air. When you're doing some abdominal training your lower back is being trained as well. You want to do multi-dimensional, multi-planed movements that prepare you for what's going to happen on the field.

It's critical to learn proper lifting technique. Start with weights (or objects) that are light enough to handle with perfect technique. Don't be so concerned about how much weight you're lifting or how fast you can increase the weight on the bar. Only increase the weight as your technique allows. That's one of the real key points. The other is if you stick with a total body program, it's going to limit the number of exercises you do, which will hopefully avoid over-training.

▲ Think "quality before quantity." That is, perfect your technique with manageable amounts of weigh. Then increase the weight as proper technique will allow.

One of the problems with weight training is that people go into the weight room and try to do fifty-three different exercises—six for this body part and six for that body part—and they start breaking their workouts into body parts instead of training the entire body. Before you know it, you've got a nagging injury because the body can't recover in time. One of the key points in avoiding lower back injury is to learn proper technique. Only add weight as your technique and strength allow and always have proper spotters and safety equipment available. Otherwise, you can strain a muscle, and because of the way the body adapts, you can get into more trouble.

This brings us back to the old misleading adage of "no pain, no gain." Remember, if it hurts, don't do it. The best thing you can do is to put ice on a sore area, rest, and see your physician. Let him or her determine exactly what the injury is and what needs to be done to correct the problem.

The Legs

▲ Youngsters tend to focus too much on developing the upper body. In actuality, a strong trunk, lower back, and legs are more important for football.

Beyond the trunk and lower back the other key to successful football is the legs. Let's go back to Chris Spielman. When he played for the Detroit Lions he tore a muscle in his chest, and though he was limited in the amount of upper body work he could do, he could still train his legs. As discussed earlier, Barry Sanders attributed much of his success to leg-based strength training. I think the importance of the legs and lower body strength is overlooked by a lot of guys who "think" they're training for football. The lower body is going to carry you around the field. It's the lower body that's going to make you more explosive and faster. That's where the primary emphasis should be for the beginner, the intermediate, and even the advanced player.

Circuit Training

There's a lot of talk in training circles today about "circuit training." This is a program in which you do a series of activities with short rest intervals between each activity. You can do circuit training in the weight room where you set up different stations and have a predetermined amount of weight at each station. You go to the station, do X number of repetitions, take a short rest, and move to the next station. Circuit training is not confined to the weight room, as versions of circuit training can also be done on the practice field. For instance, your coaches might set up an agility station. After you go through it you get a short rest, and then you move on to, say, a power station.

The benefit of circuit training in the weight room is it helps develop a base of strength and endurance from which the athlete can improve. You need a certain minimum of endurance in order to lift weights on a regular basis. For many years, Al Vermeil has been the strength coach for the NBA's Chicago Bulls. I had a chance to go visit him once when he was in the process of working with some basketball players that the Bulls had signed. The players were all from South America or Europe. They were 6'10" to 7' tall, but none of them had ever done any type of training. They came in with such poor strength foundations that when Al would try to do a weight workout with them they were done for the day after one or two sets.

So Al decided he had to build a foundation before he could get into real

> *The benefit of circuit training in the weight room is it helps develop a base of strength and endurance. . .*

▲ Circuit training, featuring an array of exercises such as these dumbbell presses, in a set amount of time can be very effective.

strength training. He set up circuit drills using medicine balls to build up their endurance and their capacity. Circuit training is best for the first time athlete, or like the basketball players above, an athlete who has never had a strength training program. It's also an excellent method to use if you're really limited in terms of time, equipment, and resources. All you have to do is a circuit of push-ups, sit-ups, etc.

Dave Redding, a good friend of mine, is the strength and conditioning coach for the San Diego Chargers. Dave has been in the NFL for years and has a great circuit training pro-gram that he does with a pair of 20-pound dumbbells. Twenty pounds doesn't sound like much when you're talking about 300-pound offensive linemen, but this program of ten exercises really works them. He'll have his players do fifteen repetitions of each exercise without ever setting the dumbbells down. For about three minutes you're going non-stop with 20 pounds in each hand doing these exercises. The moves are as simple as a set of overhead presses followed immediately by a set of bent-over rolls. Follow that with a set of lateral raises, followed by a set of walking lunges. Then do a set of standing deep knee bends or squats, and you could incorporate anywhere from four to ten exercises using light weights and a variety of repetitions. You finish that set and you rest for two or three minutes and then you do another set. You're developing the entire body in that type of a sequence.

Obviously, that's for NFL players. For junior high and high school players we're not talking about 20-pound dumbbells. We're talking about a couple of pounds—maybe 5 pounds. Whatever your level, a circuit allows you to get your heart rate up, get your muscles working, get the tendons, ligaments, and everything warmed up so that the body is prepared for the activity to come.

Make It Fun

Anyone who walks in to start a weight training program walks in with desire in his hip pocket. But the program should be fun, simple, and show some results. By fun, I don't mean a lot of horseplay. If you're doing something you really feel good about then it's a fun activity and you'll look forward to it. I try to include activities that are just plain fun. For instance, every now and then I might have my guys play Ultimate Frisbee™. In the past, I've even created team competitions.

> **When weights aren't available or perhaps aren't an option, there are alternatives.**

The first activity was a free throw in the weight room. We used one of those soft foam mini-basketballs, and each guy got three shots and we recorded the total number of conversions. If only six guys showed up that day for workouts then only six guys got to shoot free throws. We took the total amount of free throws that were made and then we awarded points. We also had a grip strength competition. At least once a week we'd take a 110-pound pair of dumbbells and we would see who could pick those up and hold them in their hands the longest. So we incorporated little things that were going to aid performance down the road, made it a team activity, and gave them a reward for their participation.

Again, I'll say, "make it fun." There are times when you need to be disciplined and focused, and then there are times when you can break up the monotony by incorporating other semi-related activities like who can do the most push-ups or who can do the most sit-ups. It adds to individual strength, but it also adds group strength, unity, and leadership.

Ultimately, it will be the combination of body weight plus free weight that will give you optimum results.

As we've discussed, sometimes you're not ready for weights. At other times you can't work with heavy weights because of an injury. When weights aren't available or perhaps aren't an option, there are alternatives.

If you're motivated enough to prepare yourself for your sport, you could sit down and put together a schedule that involves body weight exercises—primarily push-ups, sit-ups, dips, and chin-ups—and do them in an organized fashion. You could also add leg work—such as walking lunges for 100 yards or body weight squats (100 repetitions). In fact, I've done quite a bit of productive non-weight work with linemen.

Adrian Crook, a movement and flexibility specialist, has worked with John Carney, who used to be the placekicker for the San Diego Chargers. I once brought him in to help with the flexibility of some of our players. Jeff Hartings—currently the starting center for the Pittsburgh Steelers—was one of the guys who really bought into Adrian's flexibility program. At one point, Jeff had a knee injury and was not able to squat or do leg presses without pain. So in lieu of weights he just did "stances." He would spread his feet a little bit wider than shoulder-width apart and bend his knees and stay in that bent-kneed position for thirty seconds, one minute, two minutes. Adrian would work on him in the exact position he wanted him in. He might do a crossover stance and maintain that position for thirty seconds to a minute. There are always ways that you can train your body without weights if you take the time to get organized, disciplined, and do a regimen. While the results will not match those of people who work conscientiously with weights, body weight exercises can definitely train you to handle your body weight better. Ultimately, it will be the combination of body weight plus free weight that will give you optimum results.

Buying Weights

My first recommendation is simply to buy used equipment—the minimum amount you need to suit your routine for six weeks. Too many people I know have bought mountains of equipment, and two weeks later they're hanging their laundry on it. Start off with just a barbell on your garage floor. If you're disciplined enough to exercise with it two or three days a week for six weeks *then* go ahead and

▲ When buying a weight set, make sure that you have a bar capable of handling additional weight.

add a piece of equipment. If you go buy a weight set, make sure that you have a good bar that is capable of handling additional weight. Maybe you only need 150 pounds right now. Over the years you can add 10 pounds a month or so as your strength increases. Buy the minimum.

The minimum could be just one barbell. It could be one dumbbell. It could be a pair of dumbbells. I think that you're going to be limited by how much space you have, the strength of the surface that you'll be lifting on, and the amount of money that you're willing to spend. Still a 14- or 15-year-old beginner shouldn't need five or six pieces. If you can use one barbell and get results from that, then do it.

Those of you who have actually seen a weight room know that there are many kinds of weights. There are old-fashioned free weights, universal gyms, and even "weightless" units that use tension instead of actual weight.

> *. . . the ideal instrument to use if you're trying to develop real joint integrity is free weights.*

A free weight is a barbell or dumbbell with portability. This free standing advantage means you can take it anywhere you want. Generally, the distinction between free weights and a universal weight system is that free weights force you to use your "stabilizing" muscle groups—the muscles that surround your joints. These muscles are called on to help you stabilize and balance free weights. An example: In a free weight curl, the left arm is required to do just as much work as the right arm in order to keep the bar balanced. With the universal system (machines), the weight is pulled by rods or cables. Since the weight is "guided" or already balanced, the only force the athlete has to apply is enough to push or pull the weight stack. Since the weight is balanced for you, the stronger muscles can do most of the work, meaning the weaker muscles might not develop as quickly.

In the last couple of years the industry has come out with machines that give you that "unbalanced" feeling so you're forced to use the stabilizing muscles to balance and control what you're doing. Generally, people use a combination of free weights and machines. You get the benefit from the machine of being able to develop the prime movers a little bit more without a risk of injury. Meanwhile, using the free weights helps you keep and maintain the stabilizing muscle groups. Obviously, the ideal instrument to use if you're trying to develop real joint integrity is free weights.

If I'm training someone for the sport of football, I could get by with a barbell and a rack. Maybe I'd put a bench in there, but that's all. For training groups of people, especially large groups, the machines do work out a little bit better because you're trying to get more people through in a hurry. For my dollar though, if I'm trying to develop power—the key factor in football—I'm going to work primarily with free weights. The younger you are the more this is true, as free weights will allow you to fully develop your stabilizing muscles.

Weight Room Etiquette

For every setting in life—whether it's the classroom, the dining room, or a party—there's an acceptable way of acting called etiquette. For instance, in the classroom when you have a question or think you know the answer, you don't shout it out, you raise your hand. At the dinner table you don't reach across the table for the pepper, you politely ask your neighbor to pass it.

So it is in the weight room where there is acceptable courtesy and etiquette. When going into a weight room to work out, make sure your attire is appropriate for the activity. Bring a towel with you in case you per-

> *. . . weight room etiquette just comes down to treating other people the way you'd want to be treated . . .*

spire on the equipment. If you do leave some sweat behind, wipe it off immediately. Replace your weights. Even if they weren't in the right place when you got them, put them back where they are supposed to go when you're finished. When you finish an exercise, if somebody is waiting, offer to let them work in with you. That's part of the fellowship that goes along with weight training in a public gym or even in a gym where it's just other athletes. To me, weight room etiquette just comes down to treating other people the way you'd want to be treated and leaving the weight room environment the way that you would want it if it was your own personal gym.

Not everyone is always attentive to weight room etiquette. When Danny Owens played for the Lions, he would always leave a 5- or 10-pound plate on the floor. One day, when the weight room was full of players, I saw Danny leave some weights on the floor when he moved on to the next station. I turned off the music that was playing, and suddenly there was silence. Everybody turned to see what I was doing, and I said, "I've got an announcement to make: When you finish with your weights just leave them on the floor. I'll come by and pick them up later. Repeat: Just leave your weights on the floor. I'll take care of them for you." Then I turned the music back up. Everybody knew exactly whom I was talking to. Danny walked over, picked up his weights and put them away. That was the last time he ever messed up my weight room.

Today, Danny owns his own gym in Atlanta. Recently, I was passing through town, and I went to see him. Soon after I walked in I dropped a couple plates on the floor. He thought it was pretty funny. The point is, that you have to be respectful not only of your peers but also of the people who run the facility.

Playing Music

I mentioned in that little story that I turned the music down before I made the announcement. Where does music fit in with weight room etiquette? It all depends on the culture that you're dealing with. I grew up with no music allowed in the weight room, but today a lot of you are coming out of environments where music is important and you may even believe it helps you perform. It's been interesting to watch over time. The music is getting louder and more progressive. I now have players who want to come in at 6:30 in the morning to avoid all the music.

The problem is that even if everybody wants music, not everyone likes the same styles. I had fun with that in Detroit. I told them I'd play anything but real hard rap with bad language and whiny country music. In college, whoever did the most sit-ups got to determine what was on the radio. If you came in and you did twenty-five sit-ups then you got to determine what radio station the group listened to. If somebody else came in and did twenty-six he got to pick the next selection.

Time Committment

Try to keep the weight training portion of your workout down to no more than an hour from warm-up to completion. I like to keep it at ninety minutes or so even for NFL players. You keep it short and productive by excluding unnecessary exercises from the program. For instance, I'm not interested in a player doing isolation exercises for his biceps. However, I will throw a few sets of curls in

> *Avoid exercises that require an endless number of coaching points.*

there because, when an athlete can see development of his biceps, that's going to motivate him. It's going to spur him to keep working on some of these other muscles that may not develop quite as fast. But as far as the overall program, the only way you can keep it productive is to feature multi-joint exercises and keep it brief.

Avoid exercises that require an endless number of coaching points. One or two coaching points should be enough for the exercises we do. Remember, an hour and a half in the weight room is the maximum per day for the typical NFL player. If you can't get it done in that time frame you're wasting time. For younger guys I would keep it down to an hour, three times a week, and limit your workouts to between thirty and forty-five minutes of weight lifting activity. After all, the strongest men in the world train with heavy weights but do few repetitions and allow a lot of rest between sets.

Early in my training program I may only give you one minute to ninety seconds between sets. Then six weeks later I may go three minutes between sets. When I'm giving you that short rest we may be doing ten exercises in thirty minutes. Then we may switch to doing five exercises in thirty minutes. I'm going to determine the intensity based on how much time I have to train you and how much rest I give you between sets.

> **Know what your program is going to be for the day . . .**

A lot of guys who are very focused and well-intentioned wonder why they have to limit their weight room sessions. I used to coach a guy named Cory Schlesinger, who still plays for the Lions. He's a fullback from Nebraska now in his ninth year in the NFL. Cory was almost cut four years ago, and it had nothing to do with his weight room ability. The guy was strong as an ox—one of the strongest running backs we had. The problem was that he spent so much time in the weight room that he was always stiff. He couldn't turn to catch a pass out of the backfield because he couldn't keep his hips going in one direction and turn his upper torso. So I talked to Cory and convinced him to back off the weight room workouts and spend a little more time on flexibility.

Tips for Your Workout

Prepare Mentally

The night before you go to the weight room figure out exactly what you want to get accomplished. If I'm 14 to 15-years-old and I know I'm working out tomorrow, I would just start off by asking myself: "Last week I did 100 pounds on the bench press. I'm going to do seven repetitions tomorrow. What time am I going to get there?" Know what your program is going to be for the day, including what exercises you'll be doing from warm-ups through cool-down.

Imagine you were going fishing tomorrow. You wouldn't wait until morning to get ready. You would get your tackle box and your fishing rod out so that when it's time to make the journey it's an easy trip. I keep coming back to Spielman, Owens, and Spindler. They prepared themselves the day before for what they were going to do tomorrow. Nothing happened by chance. It happened by design and by preparation. One reason those three players were successful is that they developed that dedication at an early age and carried it through into high school, college, and the professional game. They didn't just wake up and say, "Oh, I've got weight training today." They prepared.

> *Even if you're new to weight training, you should be on a schedule.*

Prepare Physically

So you're mentally prepared, now the next "do" is to make sure you're physically prepared. Understand and be aware of the fact that what you do today is going to affect your workout tomorrow. You need to eat a decent dinner, get a good night's rest, and then eat breakfast in the morning.

Even if you're new to weight training, you should be on a schedule. You should have a general schedule so you know, "This is where I'm going to start, and this is what I want to do next week." You should have a plan with you at every workout.

Then once you get to the weight room it's just a matter of following the plan. Make sure that you get through your workout and maintain your focus. Do the mental/physical preparation before you arrive, and then once you're there just follow through.

Be Focused

Use visualization. That is, in your mind's eye, see yourself doing something before you actually do it. Before you get under the bar or before you pick up that barbell, try to see yourself doing that particular lift just prior to doing it.

If you can visualize yourself doing something, it puts you in a positive state of mind before you ever attempt it. There's a lot to be said for mental rehearsal and mental preparation, especially if you're in a competitive environment. It's really important to see yourself being successful even before attempting something.

Personally, I don't think there's anything magical about it. Even if you need charts illustrating the technique or need to play a tape beforehand, you can put yourself in that situation just by closing your eyes and seeing it happen. It prepares you for future success.

Using lunging, jerky movements to try and squeeze one last repetition out of a set is a surefire way to get hurt.

Use Proper Technique

Make sure you use techniques prescribed in this book or follow the instructions of a qualified coach. Using lunging, jerky movements to try and squeeze one last repetition out of a set is a surefire way to get hurt.

Wear the Right Clothing

Your clothing is going to depend upon your training environment. If you're somewhere that's cold, be sure to wear a little bit more clothing to stay warm throughout your workout. If you're in a warmer environment, you can get by with a T-shirt and a pair of shorts.

Personally, I prefer loose clothing. Some players like to wear clothing—a shirt, brief-style underwear or even a jock strap—that provides more support. It's really just personal preference. I wear athletic clothes that are fairly loose, but not sloppy. No street clothes.

Keep a Journal

Keep a journal documenting your workouts. Make sure you write down your sets and your reps everyday because you can't always remember between workouts how much weight you were lifting and how many repetitions you did. Your journal is going to be your road map for success. It will help keep you focused and on target for what you're trying to get accomplished. You can practice keeping a journal by making notes on the journal pages in the back of this book.

> *Keep a journal documenting your workouts. Make sure you write down your sets and your reps everyday . . .*

Warm Up

Warm up prior to any strenuous activity. I generally recommend doing two types of warm-ups—a *general* warm-up, and an *exercise-specific* warm-up. A general warm-up gets the overall body temperature up and loosens ligaments, tendons, and muscles. If you have no equipment available, find a rope and skip rope for three to five minutes. You can do it a minute at a time with thirty seconds of rest in-between, or you can do it for three minutes straight. It just depends on your conditioning level.

Do your warm-up until you break a light sweat on the surface of the skin. Sweat is a signal that your body temperature is elevated. But remember, warm-up needs to be done at a light enough exertion level to allow you to get through ten minutes without sapping your energy.

Once your body temperature is elevated, the last five minutes or so of the warm-up should be dedicated to light stretching. It depends on the activity that you're going to do but the stretching should involve some real light flexibility movements for the hamstrings, the lower back, the calf, the Achilles, and the shoulders. Ideally, you'd like to do a total body warm-up/stretch because most of the workouts you should be doing are total body workouts.

An exercise-specific warm-up relates to the exercise that you're going to perform. For instance, if the squat is the first exercise of the day, you might want to start with the bar (no weights) and do eight to ten squat reps just to loosen up for the squat movement. Then start adding weight for a couple more warm-up sets before doing a workout set.

In football, you also want to make sure that the neck, the lower back, and the shoulders are all warmed up prior to starting.

I think you'll find that you're going to need to stretch your legs and the lower body a little bit more. Since they are large muscle masses, they require a little more time to get loosened up. For instance, you definitely want to do something to loosen up the hamstring, the quadriceps in the leg, the calf muscle, the Achilles tendon, and the ankles. In football, you also want to make sure that the neck, the lower back, and the shoulders are all warmed up prior to starting.

During stretching exercises many of you will be tempted to bounce or move quickly, perhaps in the hope that the more quickly you perform a stretching exercise the more quickly you'll warm up. This is a mistake. You want to do static stretches where you really ease into it. When, on a particular stretch, you feel like you've reached the end of your range of motion don't stretch any further. Try to hold it for a ten- or fifteen-second count, breathing real easy. Breathing is very important when it comes to stretching. You need to control your breathing—inhaling and exhaling. If you're in the middle of doing a stretch and you hold your breath, it's going to force your muscles to tighten up and you'll be actually working against what you're trying to get accomplished when you stretch.

When I'm coaching players through stretching techniques, when they extend into a stretch, I like them to go through a slow, easy exhale—almost a martial arts style of breathing. When you've run out of air to blow out and you're ready to inhale again, then come out of the stretch. That does two things for you. First, since you only need to hold a particular stretch for anywhere from ten to twenty seconds, it keeps you in the stretch for as long as you need to be there. Second, by continuing to breathe, you avoid tightening the muscles you're actually trying to stretch.

Here's an example of the mechanics of a stretch. Sit down and spread your feet, keeping your knees locked and your toes up in the air. Reach over to your right leg with both hands, *take a deep breath*, and as you *exhale*, stretch down towards the leg, *slowly* moving your head towards your knee. Only go down to the point where you *feel* you've stretched far enough. You'll feel tightness in the back of your thigh—the hamstring. Once you've run out of air to exhale, *relax*, *breathe* back in, and come back up to the starting position. Then reach over to the left leg and perform the same type of stretch— *deep breath*, *reach*, *exhale* as you go into the stretch. Once you feel the leg start to get tight, *stop*. *Relax* and come back out of the stretch.

Some athletes like to stretch not only prior to a workout but between sets as well. I don't usually recommend that for elementary or high school athletes. I don't want youngsters to have too much to think about. I would rather have you focus on technique and simply let you recover between sets. Recovery is an important part of the process. It basically means rest. Depending upon how much equipment there is and how many athletes there are at a workout, there might be three to five guys at a station. A guy steps in and does his set of repetitions. When he's finished, he gets up while another athlete sits down to do his set. That time spent doing nothing is called recovery.

Recovery

The amount of recovery time needed between exercises is really going to depend upon what you're trying to get accomplished during that phase of training. If I have someone doing lighter weights and higher repetitions with fewer rest intervals (very much like circuit training), then I'm trying to improve their endurance ability. If I have them doing fewer repetitions but with heavier weights, I'm trying to develop more strength and I'll give them more recovery time. So the amount of recovery time should depend upon the type of program, how many exercise you're doing, and, of course, the total amount of time in that workout.

> *. . . recovery time needed between exercises is really going to depend upon what you're trying to get accomplished . . .*

I encourage you to do some form of stretching after your workout, even if it's just a five-minute stretch. By taking a few minutes and doing some easy stretching, it's going to enhance the recovery from the work that's just been completed. It helps get the waste products that are in the muscle out into the bloodstream so that the recovery process starts a little bit faster. The benefits of post-workout stretching are a reduction in soreness and an increase in your ability to come back harder and sooner. So I highly recommend a light stretch after working out.

Don't Overdo It

The primary goal here is to prepare to be a better football player, not set records. If you sit down with a strength coach and map out a program that will prepare you for football success, it's going to be based on some realistic goals and expectations—percentages of your maximum. Keep your sets and reps within those ranges or a range that you know you can handle. If you're having a real super day, maybe you can add a little weight, but by and large stick to the plan. You will still show results and you're far less likely to get hurt.

When I was studying for my masters degree at Auburn University, I went through these physiology classes where we went all the way down to the individual cell level to determine what goes on in the body when you're training. Really what it comes down to is your body's ability to handle the stress that's imposed upon it and its ability to recover from that stress. A lot of factors will affect the ability of your body to recover effectively: rest, nutrition, relationship with family, relationship with teammates—all these things affect your ability to recover. Obviously, everybody has different stresses in their lives, so everybody recovers from training and from illness a little bit differently. When I set up a program I try to give athletes a range—an upper and a lower limit—to train within. If you recover from the stress and feel good, try to stay in the upper end of that range. If you come in and you're having a bad day or there's a lot happening in your life (or you haven't fully recovered from the last training session), then work out at the lower end of the range. The range is determined for a reason, and it's important to stay within it.

> *. . . everybody recovers from training and from illness a little bit differently.*

Flexibility and Speed

As I've said, all this stretching and flexibility is primarily intended to reduce the risk of injury. It may have broader benefits as well. For instance, it makes sense that if somebody has improved flexibility, their movement should be easier, and therefore they should actually be able to run faster. I wish I could say my experience has told me this is true. There are some guys who aren't very flexible who can run like the wind, while there are others who are very flexible yet couldn't run out of sight in a day.

That being said, there is one area of flexibility that has been proven to have a direct correlation to running speed, and it's ankle flexibility. When a player learns a specific technique in running that allows him to *dorsiflex*— to lift his foot up when his leg is in an unsupported phase—there seems to be a real high correlation between that and running speed.

The dorsiflex can be practiced. The idea is simply to flex the foot up towards the shin. You can do it with no resistance, or you can do it with a partner providing light resistance on the top of the foot. There are even machines on the market that allow you to work that specific muscle group and enable you to hold that position over a longer period of time. Improving the ability to dorsiflex the foot is one way in which flexibility can directly contribute to improved speed. The other way is to improve the flexibility in the Achilles tendon. This can be accomplished through wall stretches or other stretches where you maintain the foot flat on the ground and you push the knee of that foot forward,

> *. . . prepare your ligaments and tendons, making them stronger so that you can start doing weight training exercises when you get a little bit older.*

past the toes, while trying to keep the heel on the ground. Hold the position for twenty to twenty five seconds at a time. Those are the two stretches that I've seen that will definitely improve running speed.

Does Age Matter?

Age is an important factor in exercise. For those of you under fourteen, I would recommend one workout during the week that just involves light technique work—working on the speed of doing the exercise, the technique, the balance, and the coordination. For the other two workouts that week, I would focus on body weight exercises to include chins, dips, push-ups, abdominal work, flexibility, walking lunges, and things you can do with your body weight to get in better physical condition. Basically I would try to prepare your ligaments and tendons, making them stronger so that you can start doing weight training exercises when you get a little bit older.

With the fourteen-plus age group, I recommend adding weight to the technique. Two days a week should involve weight training, adding a little bit of weight to the bar as you get stronger. Then one day a week I'd suggest body weight exercises.

ChapterFour

Weight Training

The first thing you need to do for weight training is get a journal. As I mentioned earlier, this will help keep you on track. It's going to give you a written record of where you've been and what you've done. It's important to keep an accurate record of the weight and the repetitions you've performed for each exercise in each workout. Do not include an exercise or a repetition in your journal unless it was performed with perfect form. I'd rather you come up a rep or two shy of the goal knowing that all the reps you did were on form.

In your journal, at the very bottom, leave a spot for notes. Each day you should record your body weight and note whether you felt good that day or if you had anything that was irritating you or bothering you physically. That way as you track your progress you can see how or why you slowed down at various points in your program. You don't need to put a lot of time or thought into it, you can just write "felt kind of good today, didn't feel good today, had a great workout, had a head cold," etc.

Proper Breathing

I've already discussed the importance of proper breathing when doing stretching exercises. It's no different during actual weight training—breathing plays a key

Coaches Tip

Track 17

▲ Breathing correctly during a strength training exercise is as important as the exercise itself.

role in performance. You've probably heard of the basic idea of exhaling when you're in a straining phase of a lift. Only when I'm working with the most advanced athletes and lifters do I actually train them to hold their breath. When I'm teaching youngsters, I'll start off teaching them to exhale on the part where they're extending, and then once they've brought the bar back down I instruct them to take a deep breath and then exhale again on the next extension.

The reason I teach kids not to hold their breath is that when you hold your breath during a moment of exertion you can suffer what is called a Valsalva maneuver. That's where the pressure of the lift and the held breath gets exerted against a vein in your neck and it can cause you to black out. That's why the medical community has always told weight lifters to exhale when in a straining phase.

Picking the Right Amount of Weight

Coaches Tip

Track 21

The key is to start light. The best way to pick the proper weight is to start with an empty bar. Then simply add a little bit of weight for two or three sets until you find a particular weight with which you can still execute the rec-

> In the beginning only lift ▶ 60 to 80 percent of the weight you feel you can do for a given exercise. Too much weight too soon shifts the athlete's focus from technique to getting the weight lifted.

ommended number of repetitions plus two or three extra reps.

In other words, when you're just starting out, you don't want to put on so much weight that it curtails your reps. I always like the beginners to feel like they have a little extra left over after each set. That's how it should be for the first six or eight weeks. I want new weight trainers to feel like they're only lifting between sixty and eighty percent of what they feel they could do. In other words, don't push really hard early in the program. If you do too much weight too soon, your focus shifts from proper technique to simply getting the weight lifted by any means necessary.

My guess is that a lot of you will read this, rush out to the weight room, and completely ignore what I'm saying. I hope you don't, because the slow build is the best way to increase power. Think about it as though I'm trying to build you into a skyscraper. The only way you can build a big strong building is to take your time building a solid foundation. Start slowly, develop your technique, and train your body so that your ligaments and tendons can adapt to what you're doing without any type of injury. If you can establish this foundation by moving slowly, then it's going to help you to develop a lot more power down the road. Simply, it comes back to "self imposed delay of gratification."

Your coach or trainer should be aware of this slow build concept. If he's not and you feel as though he's suggesting too much weight too soon, you need to communicate that. It's the same if you're not feeling well or if something doesn't feel right as far as technique. Let the coach know. Too many times, I've been involved in situations where I had the trust and confidence of the athletes and they believed so strongly in what I was telling them or asking them to do that they didn't give me enough feedback. It's real important for communication to go back and forth from the coach or trainer to the athlete because you're working together to try to achieve the results. Don't be shy. Tell them what you're thinking and how you're feeling.

Chapter Five

General Exercises

Working the Neck

I n the game of football, you wear a helmet, so you have anywhere from six to ten extra pounds of weight that your neck has to support. With this in mind, it's essential to condition your neck to keep it strong. When something goes wrong with your neck it's a potentially serious injury, and a lot of neck injuries can be avoided.

The primary goal with the neck is to not only make it stronger but also to make it as flexible as possible. That's one reason why, when you work your neck, you want to make sure to take it through a full range of motion. You want to train so your neck becomes more flexible. So when you do

Studies have shown that ▶ neck size is not as important in preventing injury as is neck flexibility.

Neck Exercises

Track 27

take a hit, you're able to move through a range of motion without injury. Nowadays, coaches are teaching techniques where players are doing more shoulder blocks. If you go into a situation to make a tackle, make sure your head is up, so you don't make contact with the top of your head. That's where most serious neck injuries come from—getting a shot right on the top of the helmet.

When I was coaching at Texas A&M, one of our arch rival schools had a variety of neck injuries occur in one season. Every year after the season was completed, I would visit with the trainer to look at the injuries our team had sustained to discuss what could we do from a standpoint of strength training to prevent them. It was his opinion—after forty-something years in the profession—that injuries simply ran in cycles. Some years you had ankle injuries and in other years shoulders or necks. There was no real explanation for it.

Because we were talking about our opponents' rash of neck injuries, we started doing some unofficial research on what we could do to help someone prevent a neck injury. We discovered that the size of a player's neck

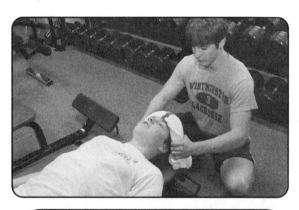

▲ The partner neck, or "towel neck," which applies resistance to neck movements, is an extremely beneficial exercise for football players.

wasn't the determining factor in whether he sustained an injury. The key was the degree of flexibility in the neck.

The number one neck exercise that I recommend is the *partner neck,* or towel neck. Get a partner. Lie down on a bench or sit in a chair. Have your partner put a towel over your head and provide resistance as you work your neck through a full range of motion: Go all the way down until your chin touches your chest, then back up in an extended position. Then do the same thing side to side for a total of ten to twelve repetitions. Your partner needs to understand that he should not be providing tremendous resistance, just enough to allow you to move smoothly.

If you don't have a partner, try manual neck work. Use a belt or a towel, holding it behind your head, providing resistance as you undergo the same motions described above. You could also lie down on a bench, fold up a towel, and put it on your forehead. Take a weight plate. I'd definitely recommend starting light—so start with a 10-pound plate. Set that on your forehead and work your neck with that resistance.

Neck flexibility is also important to incorporate into your program. If you do the partner neck exercises described above, when you finish working relax and stretch your neck for ten to fifteen seconds. Then begin working the forehead up and down. Also, work your neck for a prescribed number of repetitions. Finally, when you finish the last rep, relax again

> *. . . when you finish the last rep, relax again and stretch your neck real easy in all directions. Don't force anything.*

and stretch your neck real easy in all directions. Don't force anything. Just stretch to a point where you feel that you've gone far enough, hold for five to ten seconds, and relax.

The Shoulders

Among football players, the most popular lift of all may be the bench press. However, I think the bench press is overrated for football players interested

> ◀ **The overhead press is the best exercise for increasing overhead strength. It can be done with either barbells or dumbbells.**

in developing overhead strength. I much prefer the *overhead press*. This can be done with either a barbell or dumbbells.

For the overhead press your hands should be approximately shoulder-width. The bar should be held close to your chest underneath your chin. Knees are not locked. The legs are straight with just a slight flex in the knee so that you're in a balanced position. Your stomach should be flexed. That's going to help maintain an erect torso. As you prepare to press, take a deep breath while you've got the barbell at the chest. As you go to press the weight over head, let your head move slightly backward. Try not to turn your chin up—rather, just pull it back. Press the bar up as you're exhaling. When the barbell passes your eyes, let your head come slightly forward. Continue to press the bar until your arms are locked and the barbells are overhead.

Once you reach that position, hold it for just a half a count. Lower the bar back to the chest while moving the head backward and inhale again. With dumbbells, you don't necessarily have to move the head out of the way because there is no bar approaching your chin. I like to see the head stay parallel with the ground. That helps you maintain a balanced position. When you start cocking your head back and turning your eyes upward that puts you in an unbalanced position.

How does the ability to lift a large amount of weight over your head translate into on-the-field performance for a football player? When you're doing an overhead press, it's a multi-jointed movement. You're working the shoulders, the triceps, and the trapezius. The trapezius ties into the neck, so you're training that entire upper body area, bringing it all together. There is no doubt that overhead strength carries over to the football field when you need to take on blockers or make a tackle.

The Chest

If you're interested in developing your chest, then the *bench press* is your exercise. At this time, it seems to be the most popular weight exercise in the world. That's interesting because it wasn't even developed until the late 1950s or early 1960s.

▲ **For the bench press, when you lie down on the bench, your eyes should be directly under the bar.**

Until then most people—especially athletes—determined their strength level by how much weight they could pick up off the floor and press overhead.

Bench Press

Track 13

As I said, I believe the bench press is overrated, but if you want to make it meaningful for football, I would suggest closer hand spacing on the barbell than what you'd see power lifters use. **One particular technique I want to stress is placing your hands in a position so that when the barbell is touching the chest, your elbow is directly underneath your wrist.** In other words, your forearms are perpendicular to the floor. That position is best perfected by using an empty barbell, laying it on the bench, and working the technique. Again, for those of you fourteen and under, don't put any weight at all on the bench press, simply focus on the technique. Older players should start with just the barbell.

▲ **The extended position of the bench press should be with the bar over the chest, not the eyes. This will prevent rotator cuff injuries.**

Once your technique is perfected, then you can add weight to the bar.

When you lie down on the bench, your eyes should be placed directly underneath the bar. Take your grip—it's going to be approximately shoulder-width. Your feet should be flat on the floor, hips and upper back in contact with the bench, and you want your ankle pretty much underneath your knee.

Take a deep breath. The spotter is then going to hand the weight out so that it's directly over your shoulders. Lower the bar to your chest, making sure that your elbow is underneath your wrist. You want to touch your shirt, but not your chest, with the barbell. Bring the bar down, maintaining a tight position. In other words, your muscles are flexed as you bring the weight to your chest. Then exhale as you start to push the bar up.

Now here's an important point that a lot of young guys miss on the bench press. Once that barbell has touched your shirt and barely grazed your chest you drive the bar up and start to exhale. As the bar goes up, you need to make sure you drive with your legs. If you execute the lift properly, you are actually going to slide just a little bit back towards the head-end of the bench. As you go up in weight and the weight gets heavier, your body will not move but that force that you're generating with your legs will be transferred to the bar and the bar will go up faster and with more force.

If you want to improve your bench press, it's important that you develop your abdominals and your lower back because that will allow the force that's created through the legs to be transferred through the midsection, to the arms, and up through the bar. If you have a weak midsection, the force that you create through your legs is going to get absorbed in your midsection and will never reach the barbell.

Caution: When I was getting my masters degree, there were some studies being done— biomechanical studies on the bench press and the path of the barbell— for world class power lifters. What researchers found was that as the bar started up, people pushed it back so that in the end position the bar was over their eyes. As more and more people have learned that technique, there's been a greater incidence of rotator cuff injuries. Of course, you're training for football,

▲ As mentioned earlier, a spotter is always recommended. I particularly recommend a spotter for the bench press. This exercise leaves several ways for an athlete to injure himself, and a spotter reduces the likelihood of injury.

not to be a weight lifter. I would prefer you give up a five or ten pound increase to avoid an injury. Press the barbell almost straight up, keeping it over your shoulders and chest. *Do not push the barbell back over your eyes.*

Also important: *You really do need a spotter for the bench press, whether you have weights on the bar or not.* The biggest risk is that on a conventional bench the barbell is behind your head when you lie down. That position offers you no leverage if you attempt to take the bar off the rack. I've seen guys strain their shoulders because they were trying to take off a heavy weight and were in a bad position leverage-wise. I highly rec-ommend that a spotter (or spotters) hand you the weight and then be avail-able as you're doing the exercise.

The Legs

As you know, the game of football is played on your feet. It's important to have strong legs, and when we talk about strong legs we start at the bottom and move up: feet, ankles, calves, quadriceps, hips, lower back, abdominals. Even though we're talking legs here, abdominals and lower back play a big part in how your legs function. Of course, the legs do a lot. They give linebackers and linemen leverage. They give running backs the ability to change direction. And they give receivers and defensive backs quickness.

▲ **The squat is one of the most effective strength training exercises a football player can do.**

The Squat

One reason I really like the squat is that it involves a tremendous amount of muscle tissue throughout the body. In the early 1980s, Auburn University did a study on the benefits of the squat. In short, they studied three different physical education classes. Prior to starting the program, they tested all three groups in a squat and a bench press and recorded those numbers. Then they took one group and just let them do squats for six weeks. Another group just bench-pressed for six weeks, and then the third group did a combination of bench press and squat for six weeks. At the end of that study, what they found was that the students who had only done the bench press got stronger on the bench press but their squat performance went down. The guys who did the combination—both the squat and the bench—improved somewhat.

Low Bar Squats

Track 3

But what was really amazing is the guys who just did squats, their squat numbers went up but so did their bench press, and they hadn't bench pressed in six weeks.

The conclusion of the study was that the squat affects a huge muscle mass in your body. It probably affects more muscles than any other single lift. It really stimulates your central nervous system and makes your entire body grow. I've taught programs where guys wanted bigger arms, and I'd tell them they've got to squat. If a guy wants a bigger chest, he's got to squat because the squat affects the largest muscle mass. It helps your body produce the most testosterone, which also helps your body produce growth hormones. The squat really is the king of lifts.

The first thing to do for a squat is get the grip right. The correct grip gives a balanced position.

If I could teach fourteen- and fifteen-year-olds only one weight exercise it would be the squat. The squat is when the barbell is positioned across the back of your neck and shoulders. Then you squat and use your legs to rise from the squatting position. Like the bench press, I would suggest you learn and perfect the technique before adding any weight to the bar. I've even used old broomsticks to train people. Only after my students can execute correct squat technique and stay in balance using the broomstick, would we move on to a barbell.

I normally teach a couple of different squat techniques. There's a *high bar squat* where the bar sets up on the trapezius—the top of the neck. It's really more of a squat that Olympic lifters might perform. There's also a *power squat* where the bar is a little bit lower. It rests on the rear deltoids of the shoulders, and it's just a little bit off the trapezius. There's kind of a natural groove in there that you will find as you start to work it.

High Bar Squat

Track 4

> ▲ When doing squats, the load of the barbell transfers from your shoulders to your hips and legs.

There is a difference between these two types of squats: In the high bar squat as you go down, your knees go out over your feet and your hips stay between your heels. In the power squat, the shin stays more vertical so your knees won't go out over the toes. Hips go back and down. With the power squat technique, there's going to be a slightly forward lean in the upper torso. This is because the balance position with the barbell will be over the midline of the foot. So regardless of whether it's high on your neck or low on your neck, your body is going to adjust so that you maintain a balanced position.

After you've stepped under the bar and taken your grip, you have the bar on your back/neck. Now you want to flex your abdominal muscles. You want to tighten them up because that gives you a real strong position to allow your body to handle the weight. What you're trying to do is transfer the load of the barbell from your shoulders to your hips and legs. That can only be done when you employ a strong core and a strong lower back.

Now that you've placed the barbell, take one step back with the right foot and one step back with the left foot. The fewer steps the better. You just want to go far enough where you feel comfortable that the rack is out of the way. When you're taking the barbell off the rack, make sure that you step under the bar and lift it up. Don't let your hips and feet stay behind the bar. Step under the bar and lift it straight up. Keep your feet slightly wider than shoulder width with toes pointing slightly out—ten-fifteen degrees. Don't lean forward. Then take a third step. Your eyes should be fixed straight ahead or looking down slightly. Your abdominals should be flexed. Take a deep breath. Go down until you feel that your hips are approximately parallel to the floor. Then exhale and push with your legs and stand back up. It's a pretty simple technique really. The key points on the squat? Make sure you have an even

> *. . . you're much better off training with a weight that allows you to do the prescribed number of repetitions. . .*

grip, keep your abdominals flexed, eyes straight ahead or slightly down for balance, and as you're going into the squat, feel where your weight is. Make sure it's over your feet and you're maintaining a balanced position.

You're really just doing a deep knee bend with the barbell on your back. Transfer the weight of the force from the shoulders to the back, the hips, and the legs, and descend or go down in a very controlled manner. Once you've reached the bottom, then extend or come up a little bit faster but maintain control. You don't want the barbell flying off of your back at the top of the lift, but you want to have a feeling of acceleration coming out of

▲ **For barbell work, it's important also to learn how to be a spotter.**

the bottom position. Once you can do twenty deep knee bends (using an empty bar) with perfect technique, then you're ready to move to the barbell and slowly add weight.

Your goal should be to squat your body weight for ten repetitions, but start first by just using the bar and do a higher number of repetitions. There's no reason to be in a hurry about adding weight. The amount of weight added is dependent upon your technique and how your body is responding to the particular exercise. My experience has been that you're much better off training with a weight that allows you to do the prescribed number of repetitions—and still be able to perform three or four extra—rather than load the weight on and strain all the way through the workout. It's more important that you ingrain the proper movement patterns and make the workout enjoyable. The results will come.

Ideally, you should have three spotters: one on each end of the barbell and one behind the lifter. That way if there is ever a problem, there's somebody who can take the weight and someone who can protect the lifter. It's important that you not only learn how to do this exercise but you also learn how to spot properly. Spotting also keeps you involved because if you're not a lifter then you're a spotter. There's nothing more important than letting your teammates know that you're there to support them, to spot them, and to make sure they're safe.

If you have three spotters, use them. If you have only one, make sure to use him. You're doing something that's very serious here. It's something to try to help you become better and you want to have fun doing it, but it's a very serious activity. It's important for you to develop not only as a lifter but as a spotter.

Olympic Lifts

These two lifts are precisely what their name suggests—lifts that are used in Olympic weight lifting events. The two that you should incorporate into your football training are the snatch, which is a lift that starts with the barbell on the floor. The lifter takes it from the floor overhead in one movement. The second Olympic lift is the clean-and-jerk. Here, the lifter takes the barbell from the floor to the shoulders in one movement and then presses the barbell overhead in a separate movement. Then the lifter holds it and maintains control. Again, we're training to be football players here, not Olympic weight lifters. But these two

▲ **The snatch and the clean-and-jerk are so-called "Olympic lifts" that can be beneficial to football players.**

lifts do much to improve an athlete's ability to run fast and jump high.

In my program, I include what I call "pulls." The difference between the full exercise and my pull is as follows. The full snatch would go from the

As you advance in your lifting career, you'll find yourself hitting certain points where you feel you've reached a plateau.

floor overhead in one movement. The pull version of the snatch would go from the floor to where you extend your ankles, knees, and hips. The barbell never really travels any higher than your waist or chest. It's the same with the clean movement. You might start with the barbell already off the floor

Clean Pull from Knee

Track 6

instead of starting in a classical position. Then you're going to quickly extend the body—extending the ankles, knees, and hips. But the barbell is only going to travel as far as your waist or possibly your chest.

The Back

We've discussed the chest, the shoulders, and the legs, but it's also important to train the back so that you maintain balance. As you advance in your lifting career, you'll find yourself hitting certain points where you feel you've reached a plateau. A great way to overcome a plateau is to work the opposite muscle group.

Machine Low Rows

If you don't have the equipment you can substitute a dumbbell or a barbell bent-over row. The key with any rowing motion is to maintain proper technique throughout the exercise. The big point of emphasis when you're doing any type of rolling motion is to maintain an erect trunk or flat back and flexed abdominals. That helps maintain the integrity of the trunk. Also, you really reduce the incidence of low back problems by keeping the abdominals flexed when working the back.

Hammer Iso Low Row

One Arm Dumbbell Rows

If you're going to train the right arm, brace your left knee and your left arm on a bench. Your right foot should be on the floor. Reach down with your right hand and grab a dumbbell. At this point your shoulders should be tilted with your right shoulder down. Bring the dumbbell up so that your elbow comes up and to your side. Hold your wrist almost at a ninety-degree angle to the elbow. You want to bring the right shoulder so that it's parallel with the left shoulder and parallel with the floor. From here raise the dumbbell by moving your elbow back and up.

The breathing on this particular exercise is as follows: Take a deep breath when you put your hand around the dumbbell. Exhale as you bring it up to your side. Then, as you lower it back down, breathe deeply and inhale. It's important that you keep your abdominals flexed when you're doing this exercise. This will help you maintain a strong truck position.

Lat Pulls

I see many football players who do them, but I'm not a big fan of doing wide-grip exercises. For football training, I prefer the grip to be at shoulder width. This way you're not only working back muscles, but working your forearms and biceps a little more. One point of emphasis that I really

Lat Pull-down

DVD Review

Lat pulls in which the hands are at shoulder width are far more beneficial than so-called wide-grip lat pulls. With the hands at shoulder width, you'll work back muscles, forearms, and biceps.

try to put on this particular exercise is the grip. Circle your fingers around the bar first and *then* let your hand come in contact with the bar, as opposed to laying the flat part of the palm on the bar and then wrapping your fingers around it. The reason I emphasize this is that it's an opportunity to work your grip strength in your fingers while also developing the back. So grab the bar with your fingers first and wrap your hand around it. You're not only getting some work in for your forearms, biceps, and back but also getting your grip trained at the same time.

A study by Auburn University in the early 1980s showed that you actually involve more of your lat muscles when you bring the bar down to your chest just underneath your chin. What this requires, if you're on a traditional lat pull-down machine, is to let your torso drift slightly backward to allow for the angle to pull the barbell down to touch your chest. You don't want to swing way back and jerk the weight. Everything should be in a smooth motion. Let your shoulders and torso go backward as you pull the bar down to your chest. I prefer that over the old method of pulling it down and touching it behind the head.

The Arms

If you're like most guys, arms are probably pretty important to you, if for no other reason than you like the girls to see them. You do get some arm work in when doing your lat pull-downs and dumbbell rolls. Believe it or not, the squat, when done properly and over an extended period of time, will also help to add a little more beef to your arms. But you should also do a specific exercise with the dumbbells or with barbells to help train the biceps. It's important because in the game of football, the hands and arms have become so actively involved in grabbing and pushing people—especially in line play. It's also very important for receivers, running backs, and defensive backs to be able to hang onto the ball. Strong biceps will definitely contribute to that so there are football reasons for adding it to your program.

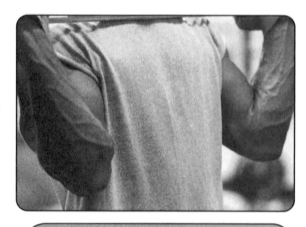

▲ **In the game of football, hand and arm strength has become increasingly important–particularly in line play.**

Arm work should occur later in the workout. It's not the primary emphasis, but I do agree that to have big biceps is definitely a motivating factor. I also realize that it is a valuable asset in playing the game of football. But don't do a lot of fancy exercises. The exercises that allow you to handle the most weight with proper technique are going to give you the most benefit.

The Bicep Curl

This is a simple exercise. Stand erect with your feet shoulder-width apart. Hold the bar with palms facing out at about mid-thigh level and parallel to the ground. Repeatedly bring the bar up in a semi-circular motion—keeping the bar parallel to the floor—from your thighs to your chest and back. Keep your elbows fairly fixed. Exhale when you're curling the weight up; inhale when you're lowering the weight. This exercise is placed towards the end of the workout because it focuses on a smaller muscle group. It simply does not require much exertion.

You can complement the bicep curl with an exercise called a reverse curl. The difference is in the position of the hands. With

Bicep Curls

Track 24

The bicep curl is best done towards the end of a strength training session because it focuses on a relatively small muscle group.

The reverse curl (note the position of the hands) works the biceps and forearm muscles.

a reverse curl, the hand is palm down and is brought up towards the bicep. The reverse curl, in addition to working the bicep, develops the forearm muscles. As I've said repeatedly, anytime that you can do an exercise that's going to involve more than one muscle group, do it. When doing these on a regular basis, the primary emphasis should be more on the reverse curl because you're working two or three muscle groups instead of just one.

Hand Strength

Not a lot of people do specialized grip work, but I think it's very important. In a football game, when you face an athlete of similar height, weight, and strength, the player with the best grip is likely to come out ahead. For grip strength, focus on an exercise that's going to train the thumb because your thumb is separated from your fingers and when you go to grab or tackle someone, the thumb is often out by itself.

I recommend an exercise called the *block toss*. Use the end of dumbbell that has the handle removed so that your fingers are on one side of the instrument and your thumb is on the other. Hold it up and release it with your left hand, and as you do, grab it with your right hand. Your fingers are on one side and your thumb is on the other, and just play toss with yourself, back and forth, dropping and catching the block, alternating hands. The thing to be careful of when first starting this exercise is you don't want the instrument to be too wide. If you train with something that is too wide and your thumb is not strong enough to handle it, you can strain a ligament in your thumb and that might take several weeks to heal. My advice is to start with something that is maybe an inch-or two-inches wide. Then as your thumb becomes stronger—you'll feel it as time progresses—you'll be able to add to the width of the object you're working with.

Another exercise is called the finger walk. Take a sledgehammer. Start off by gripping it at the naked end by pushing your fingers onto both sides. While pressing with both hands, hold one set of fingers still while your other fingers

Block Toss

Track 29

DVD Review

For grip strength, focus on an exercise that trains the thumb.

walk almost spider-like, alternating hands every four or five inches until you get all the way down to the head of the hammer.

The third type of grip strength exercise I recommend is for developing crushing grip strength. Take a pair of dumbbells—50, 60, or 70 pounds. (Advanced athletes use 100 to 110 pounds in each hand.) Then bend or squat down, pick the dumbbells up, stand straight up, and time how long you can hold them. It's a tremendous exercise for developing endurance and for developing your grip strength. Another variation of that same exercise involves a chinning bar. Reach up, wrap your fingers around the bar, close your hand around it and see how long you can hang. Your goal should be at least a minute. Once you reach a minute and a half then I would have you add ten pounds of weight and see how long you can hold that weight.

Finger Walk

Track 30

The Abdominal Muscles

You already know the importance of the abdominal muscles (abs). After all, you've heard me emphasize them over and over again. You need to develop strong abs because they are the link. The abs and lower back transfer energy from your legs up to your shoulders so that you can successfully hit or tackle your opponent and avoid injury. If you have strong abs and lower back, the energy is going to be transferred right through your body to the pads and onto the opponent. Without strong abs and lower back, the energy is lost between the legs and shoulders. It never gets to the opponent, and you are at increased risk of injury.

When training abdominals, try to keep it fairly simple. While there are many exercises to choose from, focus on these three basic exercises.

The Seated Crunch

For this exercise you can use a bench or you can do it with your back flat on the floor. In a bent knee position—holding a five-pound weight on your chest—tuck your chin to your chest. Crunch up until you feel like your lower back is starting to come off the floor. Hold it for a count and go back down. It's real easy. As you get more advanced you can add a slight turn at the top. That is,

The abs and lower back transfer energy from your legs up to your shoulders

Abdominals

Track 9

crunch up, then turn the right shoulder toward the midline, and back down. Come up, turn the left shoulder towards the midline, and back down.

The second exercise is a side bend. It can be done in a variety of ways. Stand with your feet shoulder width apart. Hold one dumbbell in your right hand with feet shoulder-width apart. Start with a light weight—a five- or ten-pound dumbbell—something that will allow you to do this exercise with relatively little strain. As you're holding the dumbbell in your hand, feet shoulder-width apart, lean your shoulders to the side of the dumbbell (your right), keeping the dumbbell close to your body. The dumbbell should go down to about mid-thigh. Then lean back to the left, raising the dumbbell up until it's about four to five inches above your waist. Then go back to the start position and repeat. The idea here is to help develop not only the lateral oblique muscles but the lower back. You'll develop a little more strength in the lower back by this turning

> The seated crunch and side bend are ▶
> terrific exercises for the abs.

side-to-side motion. Then repeat the exercise with the left hand.

The third exercise is a standing twist with weight. Stand with your feet a little bit wider than shoulder-width apart with knees slightly flexed, holding a five-pound weight at your chest. Turn to your right with your upper body till your shoulders are almostperpendic-ular to your hips. Turn back to the left and get a nice, easy rhythmic movement back and forth.

Abs Circuit

Track 11

Of course, these aren't all of the methods for training the mid-section. As you progress through your training, you will add other methods. These are just simple exercises that will help strengthen your abs for football.

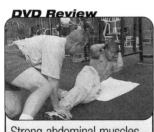

DVD Review

Strong abdominal muscles allow energy to be moved from the legs up and through the upper body. This is very valuable in blocking and particularly important in tackling.

A Word About Isometrics

I am often asked about isometrics, which first became popular in the 1950s. Isometric exercise involves pushing on an immovable object with force. What researchers found was athletes who practiced isometrics got stronger in the specific position that they were pushing but that the benefits did not extend to the athlete's entire body.

Personally, I don't recommend doing just isometrics. Isometrics might be valuable after you have begun developing some strength but not as a base part of a youngster's strength-training program.

ChapterSix

Specialized Programs

S tarting on p. 97, you will find strength training charts. These charts are a guide to following my 6 week strength training program. As we get into specific workouts, the question often arises: Should defensive backs be doing the same workout as the offensive linemen? Should offensive lineman be doing the same work as the quarterbacks? Are there specific

▲ Are there specific strength-training exercises for specific positions? At the youth level, no. As a player moves into and through high school, yes.

exercises for specific positions? At the lower levels of the game, no. As you get older and a little more experienced, there are some specialized exercises you can utilize.

Specialized exercises will be developed to help a player overcome an injury or to help compensate for a problem. My training philosophy is to combine different types of training but to keep a major emphasis that is determined by position. For the linemen (also known as "non-skill" players), the emphasis might be a little bit more on squatting. Linemen might do that two days a week and then do single leg training one day a week. Whereas the "skilled" players (quarterbacks, wide receivers, running backs, defensive backs) would squat one day and do single leg work the other two days.

Ultimately, there are some differences in the approaches for "skilled" vs. "non-skilled" players. At both the college level and the professional level there is far more specialization in training, but when dealing with players at the junior high and high school level, they're still in such a developmental stage that the basic core exercises remain the emphasis for all players. They have not developed yet to the point where there is a need for specialization.

> **Ultimately, there are some differences in the approaches for "skilled" vs. "non-skilled" players.**

This also holds true for the most specialized function on any football team—placekicking. I had Jason Hansen as a kicker in Detroit. He's been kicking in the NFL for ten years now. His first year or two with the Lions, I kept his program real simple. Coming out of college he didn't really have the strength base needed. I had to take him from that beginning to an advanced stage of basic strength before I could start doing specialization work with him.

Personally, I prefer a three-day program. Ideally, the days are Monday, Wednesday and Friday, or Tuesday, Thursday and Saturday—whatever works for the individual. The first day, I'm going to emphasize a little bit more squat and bench press with the clean pull mixed in. The second day is going to be more of a military press, as well as auxiliary legwork with step-ups. The third day, I'm going to come back and put the emphasis on the incline but still going to do a little clean pull and then a dumbbell lunge. So the emphasis for the skill players is bench and squat on Monday; overhead work and step-ups on Wednesday; and incline and dumbbell lunges on Friday. That's how it's broken down, with some auxiliaries in between.

With linemen, I'm going to focus a little bit more on heavier weights because these guys should be able to handle more work. I want to put a little bit more mass on them. So Monday's emphasis is still going to be squat and bench press. Wednesday's emphasis will be barbell presses. Then on Friday, I'm also going to have the linemen work a light squat into the incline and pull work. The overall philosophy behind this plan is that we want to train fast movements first, then move up to strength movements, followed by endurance movements and agility exercises.

Beginners

I would much rather beginners start with a program that seems almost too simplistic at first and then advance as their experience allows. I define a beginner as any athlete with three months or less of weight training experience.

With the beginner I suggest a basic three-day strength-training program that is going to work in concert with a conditioning program. I'm not going to assign specific percentages for the exercises. It's very

▲ **The best way for the beginner to determine beginning amounts of weight is to follow the clean pull section on the enclosed DVD.**

important in the beginner stage not to be too concerned with how much weight is on the bar. You want to focus primarily on correct technique. Make sure that your technique is perfect in all the exercises that you are executing.

The best way to determine the amount of weight for day one/week one of the three-day strength program for skill players or linemen is to do the clean pull from the knee. The DVD gives you an excellent explanation of how to do this exercise. Start with the barbell by itself and then add weight as you need to. Start with a weight you can comfortably perform for ten repetitions. Once you're done, set the barbell down, rest for two minutes, add about 5 or 10 pounds to the bar and then do a set of five repetitions. Take a two-minute rest, set the barbell down, and if that weight felt comfortable add another 5 to 10 pounds for one more set of five repetitions.

> **Start with a weight that's light enough to allow you to do all of the repetitions with perfect technique.**

For beginners, that's how the program unfolds. Start with a weight that's light enough to allow you to do all of the repetitions with perfect technique. Then add 5 to 10 pounds to the bar, and after a brief rest, perform one more set. With the beginner our goal is a total of three sets on the major exercises, which are the first three exercises of day one/week one. With the assisted exercises you'll have to experiment to find the right amount of weight to use. You don't want to stress too hard, but you want to be able to complete all your reps with perfect technique. You have to keep in mind that your goal is to get stronger progressively over time. In order for that to happen you need to make the proper weight selection early on that will allow you to perform all of the repetitions of each exercise with perfect technique.

While executing the beginning strength-training program (whether it be for skilled players or for linemen) take a measured amount of rest between sets. It's important to understand that the goal of the program is to improve strength. If you're going to improve strength you need to take rests between sets to allow for full and complete recovery. With the major exercises, it's generally going to be approximately three minutes from the completion of one set of squats before you perform your next set of squats. You want to make sure you follow that. I've seen quite a few athletes get stuck in training regimens and not be able to improve their strength because they forget the main purpose of the program is strength training.

The bottom line is that it's very important to rest between sets. If the weight was easy and you were able to complete all your repetitions without straining, then add 5 or 10 pounds for the next set. Also, as I stated before, it's very important to keep records of your weight training. You need to write down how much weight you are using, how many repetitions that you are able to do, and keep a record of how much rest you took between sets. As you progress from beginner to intermediate to advanced it's going to be critical for you to have these numbers to help determine your future programs.

Intermediate

The next phase is intermediate level. An intermediate is someone with three to nine months of organized weight training. At this point, you should have a good idea of the maximum amount of weight you can squat or bench press. If you don't know or don't have at least a good idea, then you should start back in the beginner program.

With the intermediate program you're still going to warm up the same way you did at the beginner level. You want at least two to three warm-up sets before you get into the actual workout. When it comes to lifting, you will use percentages that are based upon what you estimate your one repetition maximum to be in the major exercises.

For example, take the clean pull from the knee, the squat, and the bench press. By the time you're an intermediate lifter you should have some idea what your maximums are in those exercises. The purpose for giving percentages is to get you in a general weight range for the number of repetitions that you are going to be asked to do. This way you can get progressively stronger and have a better idea of how much weight to put on the bar. These percentages are strictly guidelines. When you're looking at percentages you're looking at how much, relative to your maximum, you should be lifting for a particular exercise. If you can squat a maximum of 100 pounds for one repetition then you know through experience that

▲ **Be sure to take the suggested rest period between each set of exercises. This recovery time actually speeds up the building of strength.**

75 percent of that one rep maximum is about as much weight as you will be able to do for ten repetitions. You know that 85 percent of that one rep maximum is going to be approximately what you can do for five repetitions. You know that 90 percent of your one rep maximum is approximately what you can do for three repetitions. You want to be able to set up training zones based on what your objective is, how much time you have to train,

and take into account the factors of your conditioning program. By giving you percentage ranges, I can put you in a zone to get you stronger, as well as minimize any over-training effects that might occur.

When I mentioned guesstimated maximums (above), I gave you numbers of 75 percent for a ten rep max, 85 percent for a five rep max, and 90 percent for a three rep max. Of course, 100 percent would be a one rep max. These numbers are general percentages that should work for most of the population. Occasionally you'll find an athlete who can do more than ten repetitions with 75 percent of their max. Sometimes you'll find a guy who can't do ten repetitions with 75 percent as his max. These are general guideline numbers to help provide a rough idea.

If you feel fresh and really feel good, you may add 5 or 10 pounds more than the percentage allows. On the other hand, if you didn't get enough rest, you've had an extremely stressful week, or simply don't feel very good then you may take off 10 or 20 pounds from the percentage. The important thing is that percentage gets you in a range to train within. As with the beginner, rest intervals are highly recommended. You need to adhere to those intervals. You should also continue to keep accurate records of how much weight you are lifting, how many repetitions you are performing, and the amount of rest interval you take between sets.

Advanced

Advanced lifters have at least nine months of organized weight training. The reason I've differentiated among beginner, intermediate, and advanced is to try to get the program to fit with the lifter's experience. The advanced program requires heavier weights and fewer repetitions. Therefore, technique needs to be at an advanced stage to do this program. So if I am talking about a lifter performing a squat, he understands how to place the bar on his back. He understands his body position. He understands how deep he has to go to perform a squat properly, keeping his weight balanced over the entire foot, and how to stand up and rack the weight properly.

He's still going to have to understand how to warm up properly and still

▲ You would be considered an "advanced lifter" if you had at least nine months of organized weight training.

going need two to three sets of warm-ups prior to his first workout set. I've also added to the advanced workout some "triples" and "singles" to help improve technique and to allow the advanced lifter a little more weight in his program. We'll do a variety of repetition schemes for different exercises. A triple would be a set of three. Of course, a single is just one repetition. During this six-week program, we'll go from doing a higher number of repetitions— around ten reps in week one—dropping down to eight reps in week two, six in week three, five in week four, and working our way down. At week six we're pretty much down to fives and threes, and we're handling a little heavier weight.

Again, the weight-training program in conjunction with the conditioning program is designed to take you through six weeks and prepare you for football season. Of course, you want to ensure that all exercises are performed with perfect technique; the amount of weight should not drive the program. The technique determines how much weight is going to bc on the bar. So as you complete your warm up sets and get into your workout sets, you need to make sure that you keep a record of how much weight you are lifting for each exercise. Also, note how much rest time you are taking between sets. Your journal will be your map to success as you train in preparation for the football season.

How to Get in Football Shape

STRENGTH TRAINING

The Six Week Program

Instructions

This program follows a plan that allows for three days of strength training per week. These charts are presented as one week per page, with three days of that week included on each page. Remember that I recommend forty-eight hours between strength training sessions, so you will be doing strength training about every other day.

First, you'll need to know what your estimated weight is for one repetition of an exercise. Once you have this information, you'll do multiple reps of that exercise, doing only a percentage (a portion of) that maximum weight. The strength chart for that day will tell you what percentage of weight to do for each exercise, and the number of repetitions.

The percentages noted in the charts are for major exercises in the program such as, the clean pull from the knee, the squat, the bench press, etc. "Assistive" exercises (those that can be measured not only in weight but also resistance), will not include a percentage on the chart. This is because some players will have weights or machines to work with, and others will not. Depending on what you have to work with, you may simply apply the resistance or weight that allows you to complete all of your reps without straining, and then increase the resistance or weight in small increments.

Each day's workout includes:
The name of the exercise, the percentage of weight (%) recommended for that day in the program, the number of repetitions (Rp) you should do, and the rest time (Rt) needed between repetitions. Rest time is estimated in minutes.

To find out how much weight to work with, go to the percentage chart on pp.126-127. Across the top of the chart is the maximum amount of weight you can do for one repetition of a given exercise. Follow that column down to the percentage that you need to do (as assigned in your workout schedule for that day). This will bring you to the amount of weight you should be using for that day's exercise.

An example:
Let's take Day One, Week One of the Linemen Beginner program (page 89). Determine the maximum weight at which you can do one rep of the first exercise listed, the clean pull from knee. Say your maximum is 90 pounds. Now look at the percentage of maximum weight that the exercise sheet calls for (in this case it's 40 percent). Find 90 pounds on the top of the percentage conversion chart, find 40 percent on the side and you get find 36 pounds. Now you know that for that day you are to do 10 reps of 36 pounds each followed by 2 minutes rest.

Note: If you prefer not to work with the percentage guide as a way of building your workout, you can try this method as an alternative:

For whatever exercise you are performing, start with a weight for the first set that allows you to do all of your repetitions WITHOUT STRAINING. For the second set, add a little more weight, such as 5 pounds. For the third set, add a few more pounds. You should be able to do each set without straining. It may take a little time to figure out how much weight you can do while trying to complete all of your reps and sets, but having a feel for it will work just as well as using the percentage guide.

Now it's up to you. Good Luck!

Linemen
3 Day Football Strength BEGINNER

Week 1

Day 1	Set 1			Set 2			Set 3			Set 4			Set 5			Set 6		
Exercise	%	Rp	Rt	%	Rp	Rt	%	Rp	Rt	%	Rp	Rt	%	Rp	Rt	%	Rp	Rt
Clean Pull from Knee	40%	10	2	50%	5	2	55%	5	2									
Squat	40%	10	3	50%	10	3	55%	10	3									
Bench Press	40%	10	3	50%	10	3	55%	10	3									
DB Bench	50%	10	3	55%	10	2												
Lat Pull-down	50%	10	2	55%	10	2												
Barbell Curl	50%	10	2	55%	10	1												
Neck		10	1															
Block Toss		10	1		10	1												
Ab Crunch		20	1		20	1												

Day 2	Set 1	R		Set 2			Set 3			Set 4			Set 5			Set 6		
Exercise	%	Rp	Rt	%	Rp	Rt	%	Rp	Rt	%	Rp	Rt	%	Rp	Rt	%	Rp	Rt
Barbell Military Press	40%	10	3	50%	10	3												
DB Step-Ups	50%	10	2	55%	10	1												
Low Row	50%	10	2	55%	10	1												
Barbell Shrug	50%	10	2	55%	10	1												
Reverse Curl	50%	10	2	55%	10	1												
Seated Calf	50%	10	2	55%	10	1												
Block Toss		20	1															
Knee-ups		10	1		10	1												

Day 3	Set 1			Set 2			Set 3			Set 4			Set 5			Set 6		
Exercise	%	Rp	Rt	%	Rp	Rt	%	Rp	Rt	%	Rp	Rt	%	Rp	Rt	%	Rp	Rt
Clean Pull from Knee	50%	5	2	55%	5	3	60%	5	2									
Squat	40%	10	2	50%	10	2												
Incline Barbell Press	40%	8	3	50%	8	3	55%	8	3									
DB Incline	50%	8	3	55%	8	1												
Lat Pull-down	50%	10	2	55%	10	1												
DB Curl	50%	10	2	55%	10	1												
DB Hold	Max Time 1 Set																	
Partner Neck		10	1															
Side Bend		10	1		10	1												

% = Percentage based on maximum   Rp=Rep   Rt=Rest

Linemen
3 Day Football Strength BEGINNER

Week 2

Day 1	Set 1			Set 2			Set 3			Set 4			Set 5			Set 6		
Exercise	%	Rp	Rt	%	Rp	Rt	%	Rp	Rt	%	Rp	Rt	%	Rp	Rt	%	Rp	Rt
Clean Pull from Knee	50%	5	2	55%	5	3	60%	5	3									
Squat	50%	10	3	55%	10	3	60%	10	3									
Bench Press	50%	10	3	55%	10	3	60%	10	3									
DB Bench	50%	10	2	60%	10	2												
Lat Pull-down	50%	10	2	55%	10	2	60%	10	1									
Barbell Curl	50%	10	2	55%	10	2	60%	10	1									
Neck		10	1															
Block Toss		15	1		15	1												
Ab Crunch		20	1		20	1												

Day 2	Set 1			Set 2			Set 3			Set 4			Set 5			Set 6		
Exercise	%	Rp	Rt	%	Rp	Rt	%	Rp	Rt	%	Rp	Rt	%	Rp	Rt	%	Rp	Rt
Barbell Military Press	40%	10	3	50%	10	3	55%	10	3									
DB Step-Ups	50%	10	3	55%	10	3	60%	10	3									
Low Row	50%	10	2	55%	10	2												
Barbell Shrug	50%	10	2	55%	10	2												
Reverse Curl	50%	10	2	55%	10	2												
Seated Calf	50%	10	2	55%	10	2												
Block Toss		20	1															
Knee-ups		10	1		10	1												

Day 3	Set 1			Set 2			Set 3			Set 4			Set 5			Set 6		
Exercise	%	Rp	Rt	%	Rp	Rt	%	Rp	Rt	%	Rp	Rt	%	Rp	Rt	%	Rp	Rt
Clean Pull from Knee	50%	5	2	55%	5	3	60%	5	3									
Squat	50%	10	3	55%	10	2												
Incline Barbell Press	50%	8	3	55%	8	3	60%	8	3									
DB Incline	50%	8	3	60%	8	2												
Lat Pull-down	50%	10	2	55%	10	2	60%	10	1									
DB Curl	50%	10	2	55%	10	2	60%	10	1									
DB Hold	Max Time 1 Set																	
Partner Neck		10	1															
Side Bend		10	1		10	1												

% = Percentage based on maximum   *Rp*=Rep   *Rt*=Rest

Linemen
3 Day Football Strength BEGINNER

Week 3

Day 1

Exercise	Set 1 %	Rp	Rt	Set 2 %	Rp	Rt	Set 3 %	Rp	Rt	Set 4 %	Rp	Rt	Set 5 %	Rp	Rt	Set 6 %	Rp	Rt
Clean Pull from Knee	50%	5	2	60%	5	3	65%	5	3									
Squat	50%	10	3	60%	10	3	65%	10	3									
Bench Press	50%	10	3	60%	10	3	65%	10	3									
DB Bench	50%	10	2	60%	10	2												
Lat Pull-down	50%	10	2	55%	10	2	60%	10	2									
Barbell Curl	50%	10	2	55%	10	2	60%	10	2									
Neck		10	2	55%	10	1												
Block Toss		20	2		20	1												
Ab Crunch		25	1		25	1												

Day 2

Exercise	Set 1 %	Rp	Rt	Set 2 %	Rp	Rt	Set 3 %	Rp	Rt	Set 4 %	Rp	Rt	Set 5 %	Rp	Rt	Set 6 %	Rp	Rt
Barbell Military Press	40%	10	3	50%	10	3	60%	10	2									
DB Step-Ups	50%	10	3	55%	10	3	60%	10	2									
Low Row	50%	10	2	55%	10	2	60%	10	1									
Barbell Shrug	50%	10	2	55%	10	2	60%	10	1									
Reverse Curl	50%	10	2	55%	10	2	60%	10	1									
Seated Calf	50%	10	2	55%	10	2	60%	10	1									
Block Toss		20	1															
Knee-ups		12	1		12	1												

Day 3

Exercise	Set 1 %	Rp	Rt	Set 2 %	Rp	Rt	Set 3 %	Rp	Rt	Set 4 %	Rp	Rt	Set 5 %	Rp	Rt	Set 6 %	Rp	Rt
Clean Pull from Knee	50%	5	2	55%	5	2	60%	5	2									
Squat	50%	10	3	55%	10	3	60%	10	2									
Incline Barbell Press	50%	8	3	60%	8	3	65%	8	3									
DB Incline	50%	8	2	60%	8	2												
Lat Pull-down	50%	10	2	55%	10	2	60%	10	1									
DB Curl	50%	10	2	55%	10	2	60%	10	1									
DB Hold	Max Time 1 Set																	
Partner Neck		10	1															
Side Bend		12	1		12	1												

% = Percentage based on maximum Rp=Rep Rt=Rest

Linemen
3 Day Football Strength BEGINNER

Week 4

Day 1	Set 1			Set 2			Set 3			Set 4			Set 5			Set 6		
Exercise	%	Rp	Rt	%	Rp	Rt	%	Rp	Rt	%	Rp	Rt	%	Rp	Rt	%	Rp	Rt
Clean Pull from Knee	50%	5	2	60%	5	3	65%	5	3	70%	5	3						
Squat	50%	10	3	60%	10	3	65%	8	3	70%	6	3						
Bench Press	50%	10	3	60%	10	3	65%	8	3	70%	6	3						
DB Bench	50%	8	2	60%	8	2	65%	8	2									
Lat Pull-down	50%	8	2	60%	8	2	65%	8	2									
Barbell Curl	50%	8	2	60%	8	2	65%	8	2									
Neck		10	2	60%	10	1												
Block Toss		20	2		20	1												
Ab Crunch		30	1		30	1												

Day 2	Set 1			Set 2			Set 3			Set 4			Set 5			Set 6		
Exercise	%	Rp	Rt	%	Rp	Rt	%	Rp	Rt	%	Rp	Rt	%	Rp	Rt	%	Rp	Rt
Barbell Military Press	40%	10	3	50%	10	3	60%	8	3	65%	6	3						
DB Step-Ups	50%	8	3	60%	8	3	65%	8	3									
Low Row	50%	8	2	60%	8	2	65%	8	2									
Barbell Shrug	50%	8	2	60%	8	2	65%	8	2									
Reverse Curl	50%	8	2	60%	8	2	65%	8	2									
Seated Calf	50%	8	2	60%	8	2	65%	8	2									
Block Toss		20	1															
Knee-ups		15	1		15	1												

Day 3	Set 1			Set 2			Set 3			Set 4			Set 5			Set 6		
Exercise	%	Rp	Rt	%	Rp	Rt	%	Rp	Rt	%	Rp	Rt	%	Rp	Rt	%	Rp	Rt
Clean Pull from Knee	50%	5	2	60%	5	3	65%	5	3	70%	5	3						
Squat	50%	10	2	55%	8	2	60%	6	2									
Incline Barbell Press	50%	8	3	60%	8	3	65%	6	3	70%	6	3						
DB Incline	50%	8	2	60%	8	2	65%	8	1									
Lat Pull-down	50%	8	2	60%	8	2	65%	8	1									
DB Curl	50%	8	2	60%	8	2	65%	8	1									
DB Hold	Max Time 1 Set																	
Partner Neck		10	1															
Side Bend		15	1		15	1												

% = Percentage based on maximum   *Rp*=Rep   *Rt*=Rest

Linemen
3 Day Football Strength BEGINNER

Week 5

Day 1

Exercise	Set 1 %	Rp	Rt	Set 2 %	Rp	Rt	Set 3 %	Rp	Rt	Set 4 %	Rp	Rt	Set 5 %	Rp	Rt	Set 6 %	Rp	Rt
Clean Pull from Knee	50%	5	3	60%	5	3	70%	5	3									
Squat	50%	10	3	60%	8	3	70%	8	3	75%	6	3						
Bench Press	50%	10	3	60%	8	3	70%	8	3	75%	6	3						
DB Bench	55%	8	2	65%	8	2	70%	8	2									
Lat Pull-down	55%	8	2	65%	8	2	70%	8	2									
Barbell Curl	55%	8	2	65%	8	2	70%	8	1									
Neck		10	2	60%	10	1												
Block Toss		25	2		25	2												
Ab Crunch		30	1		30	1		30	1									

Day 2

Exercise	Set 1 %	Rp	Rt	Set 2 %	Rp	Rt	Set 3 %	Rp	Rt	Set 4 %	Rp	Rt	Set 5 %	Rp	Rt	Set 6 %	Rp	Rt
Barbell Military Press	50%	10	3	60%	8	3	65%	8	3	70%	6	3						
DB Step-Ups	60%	8	2	65%	8	2	70%	8	1									
Low Row	60%	8	2	65%	8	2	70%	8	1									
Barbell Shrug	60%	8	2	65%	8	2	70%	8	1									
Reverse Curl	60%	8	2	65%	8	2	70%	8	1									
Seated Calf	60%	8	2	65%	8	2	70%	8	1									
Block Toss		20	2		20	2												
Knee-ups		15	1		15	1		15	1									

Day 3

Exercise	Set 1 %	Rp	Rt	Set 2 %	Rp	Rt	Set 3 %	Rp	Rt	Set 4 %	Rp	Rt	Set 5 %	Rp	Rt	Set 6 %	Rp	Rt
Clean Pull from Knee	50%	5	2	60%	5	3	70%	5	3									
Squat	50%	10	3	55%	8	3	60%	6	2									
Incline Barbell Press	50%	8	3	60%	8	3	70%	8	3	75%	6	3						
DB Incline	60%	8	3	65%	8	3	70%	8	1									
Lat Pull-down	60%	8	2	65%	8	2	70%	8	1									
DB Curl	60%	8	2	65%	8	2	70%	8	1									
DB Hold	Max Time 1 Set																	
Partner Neck		10	1															
Side Bend		15	1		15	1		15	1									

% = Percentage based on maximum   Rp=Rep   Rt=Rest

Linemen
3 Day Football Strength BEGINNER

Week 6

Day 1

Exercise	Set 1 %	Rp	Rt	Set 2 %	Rp	Rt	Set 3 %	Rp	Rt	Set 4 %	Rp	Rt	Set 5 %	Rp	Rt	Set 6 %	Rp	Rt
Clean Pull from Knee	50%	5	3	60%	5	3	70%	5	3	75%	5	3						
Squat	50%	10	3	60%	8	3	70%	6	3	75%	6	3						
Bench Press	50%	10	3	60%	8	3	72%	6	3	75%	6	3						
DB Bench	60%	8	2	70%	8	2	75%	8	2									
Lat Pull-down	60%	8	2	70%	8	2	75%	8	2									
Barbell Curl	50%	8	2	60%	8	2	70%	8	2									
Neck		10	2	60%	10	1												
Block Toss		25	2		25	1												
Ab Crunch		30	1		30	1		30	1									

Day 2

Exercise	Set 1 %	Rp	Rt	Set 2 %	Rp	Rt	Set 3 %	Rp	Rt	Set 4 %	Rp	Rt	Set 5 %	Rp	Rt	Set 6 %	Rp	Rt
Barbell Military Press	50%	10	3	60%	8	3	70%	6	3	75%	6	2						
DB Step-Ups	60%	8	3	65%	8	3	70%	8	1									
Low Row	60%	8	2	65%	8	2	70%	8	1									
Barbell Shrug	60%	8	2	65%	8	2	70%	8	1									
Reverse Curl	60%	8	2	65%	8	2	70%	8	1									
Seated Calf	50%	12	2	55%	12	2	60%	12	1									
Block Toss		20	2		20	2												
Knee-ups		15	1		15	1		15	1									

Day 3

Exercise	Set 1 %	Rp	Rt	Set 2 %	Rp	Rt	Set 3 %	Rp	Rt	Set 4 %	Rp	Rt	Set 5 %	Rp	Rt	Set 6 %	Rp	Rt
Clean Pull from Knee	50%	5	2	60%	5	3	70%	5	3									
Squat	50%	10	3	60%	8	3	65%	6	2									
Incline Barbell Press	50%	8	3	60%	8	3	70%	6	3	75%	6	3						
DB Incline	60%	8	3	70%	8	3	75%	8	2									
Lat Pull-down	60%	8	2	65%	8	2	70%	8	1									
DB Curl	60%	8	2	65%	8	2	70%	8	1									
DB Hold	Max Time 1 Set																	
Partner Neck		10	1															
Side Bend		15	1		15	1		15	1									

% = Percentage based on maximum   *Rp*=Rep   *Rt*=Rest

Linemen
3 Day Football Strength INTERMEDIATE

Week 1

Day 1	Set 1			Set 2			Set 3			Set 4			Set 5			Set 6		
Exercise	%	Rp	Rt	%	Rp	Rt	%	Rp	Rt	%	Rp	Rt	%	Rp	Rt	%	Rp	Rt
Clean Pull from Knee	40%	5	2	50%	5	2	60%	5	3	65%	5	3						
Squat	40%	10	3	50%	10	3	60%	10	3	65%	10	3	75%	3	2			
Bench Press	40%	10	3	50%	10	3	60%	10	3	65%	10	3	75%	3	2			
DB Bench	50%	10	2	60%	10	3												
Dips with Weight	50%	8	3	60%	8	2												
Lat Pull-down	50%	10	2	55%	10	2	60%	10	1									
Barbell Curl	50%	10	2	55%	10	2	60%	10	1									
Block Toss		20	2		20	1												
Neck		10	2	60%	10	1												
Ab Crunch		25	1		25	1												

Day 2	Set 1			Set 2			Set 3			Set 4			Set 5			Set 6		
Exercise	%	Rp	Rt	%	Rp	Rt	%	Rp	Rt	%	Rp	Rt	%	Rp	Rt	%	Rp	Rt
DB Press	50%	10	3	60%	10	3												
DB Step-Ups	50%	10	3	60%	10	2												
DB Lunge	50%	10	3	60%	10	1												
Barbell Shrug	50%	10	2	60%	10	2	65%	10	1									
Reverse Curl	50%	10	2	60%	10	2	65%	10	1									
Standing Calf Raise	50%	10	1	60%	10	1												
Neck		10	1	60%	10	1												
Knee-ups		12	1		12	1												

Day 3	Set 1			Set 2			Set 3			Set 4			Set 5			Set 6		
Exercise	%	Rp	Rt	%	Rp	Rt	%	Rp	Rt	%	Rp	Rt	%	Rp	Rt	%	Rp	Rt
Clean Pull from Knee	40%	5	2	50%	5	2	55%	5	3	60%	5	3						
Squat	40%	10	2	50%	10	3	55%	10	2									
Incline Barbell Press	40%	10	3	50%	8	3	60%	8	4	65%	8	3	75%	3	2			
DB Incline	50%	8	3	60%	8	1												
Low Row	40%	10	2	50%	10	2	55%	10	1									
DB Curl	40%	10	2	50%	10	2	55%	10	1									
Partner Neck		10	1															
DB Hold	Max Time 1 Set																	
Side Bend		15	1		15	1												

% = Percentage based on maximum   *Rp*=Rep   *Rt*=Rest

Linemen
3 Day Football Strength INTERMEDIATE

Week 2

Day 1

Exercise	Set 1 %	Rp	Rt	Set 2 %	Rp	Rt	Set 3 %	Rp	Rt	Set 4 %	Rp	Rt	Set 5 %	Rp	Rt	Set 6 %	Rp	Rt
Clean Pull from Knee	40%	5	2	60%	5	3	65%	5	3	70%	5	3						
Squat	40%	10	3	60%	10	4	70%	10	4	80%	3	2						
Bench Press	40%	10	3	60%	10	3	70%	10	4	80%	3	3						
DB Bench	50%	10	2	60%	10	3	65%	10	3									
Dips with Weight	50%	8	3	60%	8	3												
Lat Pull-down	50%	10	2	60%	10	2	70%	10	1									
Barbell Curl	50%	10	2	60%	10	2	65%	10	1									
Block Toss		25	2		25	1												
Neck		10	2	60%	10	1												
Ab Crunch		25	1		25	1												

Day 2

Exercise	Set 1 %	Rp	Rt	Set 2 %	Rp	Rt	Set 3 %	Rp	Rt	Set 4 %	Rp	Rt	Set 5 %	Rp	Rt	Set 6 %	Rp	Rt
DB Press	50%	10	3	60%	10	3	65%	10	1									
DB Step-Ups	50%	10	3	60%	10	2												
DB Lunge	50%	10	3	60%	10	1												
Barbell Shrug	50%	10	2	60%	10	2	70%	10	1									
Reverse Curl	50%	10	2	60%	10	2	65%	10	1									
Standing Calf Raise	50%	10	2	60%	10	2	70%	10	1									
Neck		10	2	60%	10	1												
Knee-ups		12	1		12	1												

Day 3

Exercise	Set 1 %	Rp	Rt	Set 2 %	Rp	Rt	Set 3 %	Rp	Rt	Set 4 %	Rp	Rt	Set 5 %	Rp	Rt	Set 6 %	Rp	Rt
Clean Pull from Knee	50%	5	2	60%	5	3	70%	5	3									
Squat	40%	10	3	50%	10	3	60%	10	2									
Incline Barbell Press	40%	10	3	60%	8	4	70%	8	4	80%	3	3						
DB Incline	50%	8	3	60%	8	3	65%	8	1									
Low Row	40%	10	2	50%	10	3	65%	10	1									
DB Curl	40%	10	2	50%	10	2	65%	10	1									
Partner Neck		10	2															
DB Hold	Max Time 1 Set																	
Side Bend		15	1		15	1												

% = Percentage based on maximum   *Rp*=Rep   *Rt*=Rest

Linemen
3 Day Football Strength INTERMEDIATE

Week 3

Day 1

Exercise	Set 1 %	Rp	Rt	Set 2 %	Rp	Rt	Set 3 %	Rp	Rt	Set 4 %	Rp	Rt	Set 5 %	Rp	Rt	Set 6 %	Rp	Rt
Clean Pull from Knee	40%	5	2	60%	5	3	70%	5	3	75%	5	3						
Squat	40%	10	3	60%	5	3	70%	5	3	75%	5	3	85%	2	3			
Bench Press	40%	10	3	60%	5	3	70%	5	3	75%	3	3	85%	2	3			
DB Bench	60%	8	2	65%	8	3	70%	8	2									
Dips with Weight	60%	8	3	70%	8	1												
Lat Pull-down	60%	8	3	70%	8	3	75%	8	1									
Barbell Curl	60%	10	3	65%	10	3	70%	10	1									
Block Toss		30	2		30	1												
Neck		10	2	60%	10	1												
Ab Crunch		30	1		30	1												

Day 2

Exercise	Set 1 %	Rp	Rt	Set 2 %	Rp	Rt	Set 3 %	Rp	Rt	Set 4 %	Rp	Rt	Set 5 %	Rp	Rt	Set 6 %	Rp	Rt
DB Press	60%	8	3	65%	8	3	70%	8	1									
DB Step-Ups	50%	8	3	60%	8	3	70%	8	2									
DB Lunge	50%	8	3	60%	8	3	70%	8	1									
Barbell Shrug	60%	8	2	70%	8	2	75%	8	1									
Reverse Curl	60%	10	2	65%	10	2	70%	10	1									
Standing Calf Raise	50%	8	2	60%	10	2	70%	10	1									
Neck		10	2	60%	10	2												
Knee-ups		15	1		15	1												

Day 3

Exercise	Set 1 %	Rp	Rt	Set 2 %	Rp	Rt	Set 3 %	Rp	Rt	Set 4 %	Rp	Rt	Set 5 %	Rp	Rt	Set 6 %	Rp	Rt
Clean Pull from Knee	50%	5	2	60%	5	3	70%	5	3									
Squat	40%	10	3	50%	5	2	60%	5	2									
Incline Barbell Press	40%	10	3	60%	5	4	70%	5	4	75%	5	4	80%	3	3			
DB Incline	60%	8	3	65%	8	3	70%	8	1									
Low Row	50%	8	2	60%	8	3	70%	8	1									
DB Curl	50%	10	2	60%	10	3	70%	10	1									
Partner Neck		10	2															
DB Hold	Max Time 1 Set																	
Side Bend		20	1		20	1												

% = Percentage based on maximum   Rp=Rep   Rt=Rest

Linemen
3 Day Football Strength INTERMEDIATE

Week 4

Day 1	Set 1			Set 2			Set 3			Set 4			Set 5			Set 6		
Exercise	%	Rp	Rt	%	Rp	Rt	%	Rp	Rt	%	Rp	Rt	%	Rp	Rt	%	Rp	Rt
Clean Pull from Knee	40%	5	2	60%	5	3	70%	5	3	80%	3	3						
Squat	40%	10	3	60%	5	3	70%	5	3	80%	5	3	85%	2	3			
Bench Press	40%	10	3	60%	5	3	70%	5	3	80%	5	3	85%	2	3			
DB Bench	60%	8	3	65%	8	3	70%	8	2									
Dips with Weight	60%	8	3	70%	8	1												
Lat Pull-down	60%	8	2	70%	8	2	75%	8	1									
Barbell Curl	60%	8	2	70%	8	2	75%	8	1									
Block Toss		30	2		30	1												
Neck		8	2	70%	8	1												
Ab Crunch		30	1		30	1		30	1									

Day 2	Set 1			Set 2			Set 3			Set 4			Set 5			Set 6		
Exercise	%	Rp	Rt	%	Rp	Rt	%	Rp	Rt	%	Rp	Rt	%	Rp	Rt	%	Rp	Rt
DB Press	60%	8	3	65%	8	3	70%	8	1									
DB Step-Ups	50%	8	3	60%	8	3	70%	8	2									
DB Lunge	50%	8	3	60%	8	3	70%	8	1									
Barbell Shrug	60%	8	2	70%	8	2	75%	8	1									
Reverse Curl	60%	8	2	70%	8	2	75%	8	1									
Standing Calf Raise	50%	12	2	60%	12	2	70%	12	1									
Neck		8	2	65%	8	2	70%	8	1									
Knee-ups		15	1		15	1		15	1									

Day 3	Set 1			Set 2			Set 3			Set 4			Set 5			Set 6		
Exercise	%	Rp	Rt	%	Rp	Rt	%	Rp	Rt	%	Rp	Rt	%	Rp	Rt	%	Rp	Rt
Clean Pull from Knee	50%	5	2	60%	5	3	70%	5	3	75%	5	3						
Squat	40%	10	2	50%	5	3	60%	5	3									
Incline Barbell Press	40%	10	3	60%	5	3	70%	5	4	80%	5	4	85%	2	3			
DB Incline	60%	8	3	65%	8	3	70%	8	1									
Low Row	60%	8	3	70%	8	3	75%	8	1									
DB Curl	60%	8	2	70%	8	2	75%	8	1									
Partner Neck		10	2															
DB Hold	Max Time 1 Set																	
Side Bend		20	1		20	1		20	1									

% = Percentage based on maximum   Rp=Rep   Rt=Rest

Linemen
3 Day Football Strength INTERMEDIATE

Week 5

Day 1	Set 1			Set 2			Set 3			Set 4			Set 5			Set 6		
Exercise	%	Rp	Rt	%	Rp	Rt	%	Rp	Rt	%	Rp	Rt	%	Rp	Rt	%	Rp	Rt
Clean Pull from Knee	50%	5	3	60%	5	3	70%	5	3	80%	5	3						
Squat	40%	10	3	60%	5	3	70%	5	4	80%	5	4	85%	3	3			
Bench Press	40%	10	3	60%	5	3	70%	5	3	80%	5	4	85%	3	4	90%	1	3
DB Bench	60%	6	3	70%	6	3	75%	6	2									
Dips with Weight	60%	6	3	70%	6	1												
Lat Pull-down	60%	6	2	70%	6	3	80%	6	1									
Barbell Curl	60%	8	2	70%	8	2	75%	8	1									
Block Toss		35	2		35	2												
Neck		8	2	70%	8	2												
Ab Crunch		30	1		30	1		30	1									

Day 2	Set 1			Set 2			Set 3			Set 4			Set 5			Set 6		
Exercise	%	Rp	Rt	%	Rp	Rt	%	Rp	Rt	%	Rp	Rt	%	Rp	Rt	%	Rp	Rt
DB Press	60%	6	3	70%	6	3	75%	6	2									
DB Step-Ups	60%	6	3	70%	6	3	75%	6	2									
DB Lunge	60%	6	3	70%	6	3	75%	6	1									
Barbell Shrug	60%	6	2	70%	6	2	80%	6	2									
Reverse Curl	60%	6	2	70%	6	2	75%	6	1									
Standing Calf Raise	60%	12	2	65%	12	2	70%	12	1									
Neck		10	1	70%	8	2												
Knee-ups		15	1		15	1		15	1									

Day 3	Set 1			Set 2			Set 3			Set 4			Set 5			Set 6		
Exercise	%	Rp	Rt	%	Rp	Rt	%	Rp	Rt	%	Rp	Rt	%	Rp	Rt	%	Rp	Rt
Clean Pull from Knee	50%	5	2	60%	3	3	70%	3	3	80%	3	3						
Squat	40%	10	2	60%	5	3	65%	5	3									
Incline Barbell Press	40%	10	3	60%	5	4	70%	5	4	80%	5	4	85%	3	3			
DB Incline	60%	6	3	70%	6	3	75%	6	2									
Low Row	60%	6	3	70%	6	3	75%	6	3									
DB Curl	60%	8	2	70%	8	2	75%	8	1									
Partner Neck		10	2	60%	10	1												
DB Hold	Max Time 1 Set																	
Side Bend		20	1		20	1		20	1									

% = Percentage based on maximum   Rp=Rep   Rt=Rest

Linemen
3 Day Football Strength INTERMEDIATE

Week 6

Day 1

Exercise	%	Rp	Rt	%	Rp	Rt	%	Rp	Rt	%	Rp	Rt	%	Rp	Rt	%	Rp	Rt
Clean Pull from Knee	40%	5	3	60%	3	3	70%	3	4	80%	3	3	85%	1	3			
Squat	40%	10	3	60%	5	3	70%	5	3	80%	3	3	85%	3	3			
Bench Press	40%	10	3	60%	5	3	70%	5	4	80%	3	4	85%	3	4	90%	2	3
DB Bench	60%	6	3	70%	6	3	80%	6	2									
Dips with Weight	60%	6	3	70%	6	1												
Lat Pull-down	60%	6	2	70%	6	3	80%	6	1									
Barbell Curl	60%	8	2	70%	8	3	75%	8	1									
Block Toss		40	2		40	1												
Neck		8	2	70%	8	1												
Ab Crunch		35	1		35	1		35	1									

Day 2

Exercise	%	Rp	Rt	%	Rp	Rt	%	Rp	Rt	%	Rp	Rt	%	Rp	Rt	%	Rp	Rt
DB Press	60%	6	3	70%	6	3	80%	6	3									
DB Step-Ups	60%	6	3	70%	6	3	75%	6	2									
DB Lunge	60%	6	3	70%	6	3	75%	6	1									
Barbell Shrug	60%	6	2	70%	6	2	80%	6	1									
Reverse Curl	60%	6	2	70%	6	2	75%	6	1									
Standing Calf Raise	60%	12	2	70%	12	2	75%	12	1									
Neck		8	2	70%	8	2												
Knee-ups		20	1		20	1		20	1									

Day 3

Exercise	%	Rp	Rt	%	Rp	Rt	%	Rp	Rt	%	Rp	Rt	%	Rp	Rt	%	Rp	Rt
Clean Pull from Knee	50%	5	2	60%	3	3	70%	3	3	80%	3	3						
Squat	40%	10	2	60%	5	3	65%	5	3									
Incline Barbell Press	40%	10	3	60%	5	4	70%	5	4	80%	3	4	85%	3	4	90%	1	3
DB Incline	60%	6	3	70%	6	3	80%	6	1									
Low Row	60%	6	3	70%	6	3	80%	6	3									
DB Curl	60%	8	2	70%	8	2	75%	8	2									
Partner Neck		8	2	70%	8	1												
DB Hold	Max Time 1 Set																	
Side Bend		25	1		25	1		25	1									

% = Percentage based on maximum   Rp=Rep   Rt=Rest

Linemen
3 Day Football Strength ADVANCED

Week 1

Day 1	Set 1			Set 2			Set 3			Set 4			Set 5			Set 6		
Exercise	%	Rp	Rt	%	Rp	Rt	%	Rp	Rt	%	Rp	Rt	%	Rp	Rt	%	Rp	Rt
Power Clean	40%	5	2	60%	5	2	70%	5	3									
Squat	40%	10	4	60%	10	4	70%	10	4	80%	3	4	90%	1	3			
Bench Press	40%	10	3	60%	10	4	70%	10	4	80%	3	4	90%	1	3			
DB Bench Press	60%	10	3	65%	10	3												
Dips with Weight	50%	8	3	60%	8	2												
Barbell Curl	50%	10	2	55%	10	2	60%	10	1									
Block Toss		25	2		25	1												
Machine Neck		10	2	55%	10	1												
Ab Crunch		30	1															

Day 2	Set 1			Set 2			Set 3			Set 4			Set 5			Set 6		
Exercise	%	Rp	Rt	%	Rp	Rt	%	Rp	Rt	%	Rp	Rt	%	Rp	Rt	%	Rp	Rt
Push Press	40%	5	2	50%	5	3	60%	5	3	65%	5	3						
DB Press	50%	8	3	60%	8	3	65%	8	2									
DB Step-Ups	50%	10	3	55%	10	2												
DB Lunge	50%	10	3	55%	10	2												
Lat Pull-down	50%	10	2	60%	10	2	65%	10	3									
Low Row	50%	10	2	60%	10	2	65%	10	3									
Barbell Shrug	50%	10	2	60%	10	2	70%	10	2									
Standing Calf	50%	10	3	55%	10	2												
Partner Neck		10	2															
Finger Walk	6 lb	3	2															
Knee-ups		15	1		15	1												

Day 3	Set 1			Set 2			Set 3			Set 4			Set 5			Set 6		
Exercise	%	Rp	Rt	%	Rp	Rt	%	Rp	Rt	%	Rp	Rt	%	Rp	Rt	%	Rp	Rt
Clean Pull from Knee	40%	5	2	50%	5	3	60%	5	3	70%	5	3						
Leg Press	40%	10	4	60%	10	4	75%	3	2									
Incline Barbell Press	40%	10	4	60%	10	4	65%	10	4	75%	3	4	85%	1	2			
DB Incline	60%	10	3	70%	10	2												
DB Curl	50%	10	2	55%	10	2	60%	10	1									
Neck Machine		10	1	55%	10	1												
DB Hold	Max Time 1 Set																	
Side Bend		20	1		20	1												

% = Percentage based on maximum   *Rp*=Rep   *Rt*=Rest

Linemen
3 Day Football Strength ADVANCED

Week 2

Day 1

Exercise	Set 1 %	Rp	Rt	Set 2 %	Rp	Rt	Set 3 %	Rp	Rt	Set 4 %	Rp	Rt	Set 5 %	Rp	Rt	Set 6 %	Rp	Rt
Power Clean	40%	5	2	60%	5	3	70%	5	3	75%	5	3						
Squat	40%	10	3	60%	8	4	70%	8	4	75%	8	4	85%	3	4	90%	1	3
Bench Press	40%	10	3	60%	8	4	70%	8	4	75%	8	4	85%	3	4	90%	1	3
DB Bench Press	60%	8	3	65%	8	3	70%	8	3									
Dips with Weight	60%	8	3	65%	8	2												
Barbell Curl	50%	10	2	60%	10	3	65%	10	1									
Block Toss		30	2		30	2												
Machine Neck		10	2	60%	10	3												
Ab Crunch		30	1		30	1												

Day 2

Exercise	Set 1 %	Rp	Rt	Set 2 %	Rp	Rt	Set 3 %	Rp	Rt	Set 4 %	Rp	Rt	Set 5 %	Rp	Rt	Set 6 %	Rp	Rt
Push Press	40%	5	3	60%	5	3	65%	5	3	70%	5	3						
DB Press	50%	8	3	60%	8	3	70%	8	1									
DB Step-Ups	50%	8	3	55%	8	3	60%	8	2									
DB Lunge	50%	8	3	55%	8	1												
Lat Pull-down	50%	10	2	60%	10	3	70%	10	2									
Low Row	50%	10	2	60%	10	3	70%	10	1									
Barbell Shrug	50%	10	2	60%	10	2	70%	10	1									
Standing Calf	50%	10	2	60%	10	1												
Partner Neck		10	1															
Finger Walk	6 lb	3	1															
Knee-ups		15	1		15	1												

Day 3

Exercise	Set 1 %	Rp	Rt	Set 2 %	Rp	Rt	Set 3 %	Rp	Rt	Set 4 %	Rp	Rt	Set 5 %	Rp	Rt	Set 6 %	Rp	Rt
Clean Pull from Knee	50%	5	2	60%	5	3	70%	5	3	75%	5	2						
Leg Press	40%	10	3	60%	8	4	70%	8	4	80%	3	3						
Incline Barbell Press	40%	10	3	60%	8	4	70%	8	4	80%	3	4	90%	1	3			
DB Incline	60%	8	3	70%	8	3	75%	8	2									
DB Curl	50%	10	2	60%	10	2	65%	10	1									
Neck Machine		10	2	55%	10	1												
DB Hold	Max Time 1 Set																	
Side Bend		20	1		20	1												

% = Percentage based on maximum   Rp=Rep   Rt=Rest

Linemen
3 Day Football Strength ADVANCED

Week 3

Day 1

Exercise	Set 1 %	Rp	Rt	Set 2 %	Rp	Rt	Set 3 %	Rp	Rt	Set 4 %	Rp	Rt	Set 5 %	Rp	Rt	Set 6 %	Rp	Rt
Power Clean	40%	5	2	60%	5	3	70%	5	3	75%	5	3	80%	3	3			
Squat	40%	10	3	60%	6	3	70%	6	3	80%	6	3	85%	2	3	90%	1	2
Bench Press	50%	10	3	70%	6	3	75%	6	3	80%	6	3	85%	2	3	90%	1	2
DB Bench Press	60%	6	2	70%	6	3	75%	6	3									
Dips with Weight	60%	6	3	65%	6	3	70%	6	2									
Barbell Curl	60%	8	2	65%	8	3	70%	8	1									
Block Toss		35	2		35	1												
Machine Neck		10	2	60%	10	1												
Ab Crunch		30	1		30	1		30	1									

Day 2

Exercise	Set 1 %	Rp	Rt	Set 2 %	Rp	Rt	Set 3 %	Rp	Rt	Set 4 %	Rp	Rt	Set 5 %	Rp	Rt	Set 6 %	Rp	Rt
Push Press	40%	5	3	60%	3	3	70%	3	3	75%	3	3						
DB Press	60%	6	3	70%	6	3	75%	6	2									
DB Step-Ups	50%	5	3	60%	5	3	70%	5	2									
DB Lunge	50%	5	3	60%	5	1												
Lat Pull-down	60%	8	2	70%	8	2	75%	8	2									
Low Row	60%	8	2	70%	8	2	75%	8	1									
Barbell Shrug	60%	8	2	70%	8	2	75%	8	1									
Standing Calf	50%	12	2	60%	12	2	65%	12	1									
Partner Neck		10	1															
Finger Walk	6 lb	4	1															
Knee-ups		15	1		15	1		15	1									

Day 3

Exercise	Set 1 %	Rp	Rt	Set 2 %	Rp	Rt	Set 3 %	Rp	Rt	Set 4 %	Rp	Rt	Set 5 %	Rp	Rt	Set 6 %	Rp	Rt
Clean Pull from Knee	40%	5	2	60%	5	3	70%	5	3	80%	3	2						
Leg Press	40%	10	3	60%	6	4	70%	6	4	75%	6	4	85%	2	2			
Incline Barbell Press	40%	10	3	60%	6	4	70%	6	4	75%	6	4	85%	2	4	90%	1	3
DB Incline	60%	8	3	70%	6	3	75%	6	2									
DB Curl	60%	8	2	65%	8	2	70%	8	1									
Neck Machine		10	2	60%	10	1	70%	10	1									
DB Hold	Max Time 1 Set																	
Side Bend		20	1		20	1		20	1									

% = Percentage based on maximum   Rp=Rep   Rt=Rest

Linemen
3 Day Football Strength ADVANCED

Week 4

Day 1	Set 1			Set 2			Set 3			Set 4			Set 5			Set 6		
Exercise	%	Rp	Rt	%	Rp	Rt	%	Rp	Rt	%	Rp	Rt	%	Rp	Rt	%	Rp	Rt
Power Clean	40%	5	2	60%	5	3	70%	5	3	80%	4	3						
Squat	40%	10	3	60%	5	4	70%	5	4	80%	5	4	85%	3	4	90%	1	3
Bench Press	40%	10	3	60%	5	4	70%	5	4	80%	5	4	90%	2	4	95%	1	3
DB Bench Press	60%	5	3	70%	5	3	80%	5	3									
Dips with Weight	60%	6	3	70%	6	3	75%	6	2									
Barbell Curl	60%	8	2	70%	8	2	75%	8	1									
Block Toss		40	2		40	1												
Machine Neck		8	2	60%	8	1												
Ab Crunch		35	1		35	1		35	1									

Day 2	Set 1			Set 2			Set 3			Set 4			Set 5			Set 6		
Exercise	%	Rp	Rt	%	Rp	Rt	%	Rp	Rt	%	Rp	Rt	%	Rp	Rt	%	Rp	Rt
Push Press	40%	5	3	60%	3	3	70%	3	3	75%	3	3	80%	3	2			
DB Press	60%	6	3	70%	6	3	75%	6	1									
DB Step-Ups	50%	5	3	60%	5	3	70%	5	3									
DB Lunge	50%	5	3	60%	5	1												
Lat Pull-down	60%	8	2	70%	8	2	75%	8	2									
Low Row	60%	8	2	70%	8	2	75%	8	1									
Barbell Shrug	60%	8	2	70%	8	2	75%	8	1									
Standing Calf	50%	12	2	60%	12	2	65%	12	1									
Partner Neck		8	1															
Finger Walk	6 lb	4	1															
Knee-ups		20	1		20	1		20	1									

Day 3	Set 1			Set 2			Set 3			Set 4			Set 5			Set 6		
Exercise	%	Rp	Rt	%	Rp	Rt	%	Rp	Rt	%	Rp	Rt	%	Rp	Rt	%	Rp	Rt
Clean Pull from Knee	40%	5	2	60%	5	3	70%	5	3	80%	5	3						
Leg Press	40%	10	4	60%	5	4	70%	5	4	75%	5	4	85%	3	2			
Incline Barbell Press	40%	10	3	60%	5	4	70%	5	4	80%	5	4	85%	2	4	90%	1	3
DB Incline	60%	5	3	70%	5	3	80%	5	2									
DB Curl	60%	8	2	65%	8	2	70%	8	1									
Neck Machine		8	2	60%	8	1												
DB Hold	Max Time 1 Set																	
Side Bend		25	1		25	1		25	1									

% = Percentage based on maximum   Rp=Rep   Rt=Rest

Linemen
3 Day Football Strength ADVANCED

Week 5

Day 1

Exercise	Set 1 %	Rp	Rt	Set 2 %	Rp	Rt	Set 3 %	Rp	Rt	Set 4 %	Rp	Rt	Set 5 %	Rp	Rt	Set 6 %	Rp	Rt
Power Clean	50%	5	3	60%	5	3	70%	5	3	80%	5	3						
Squat	40%	10	3	60%	5	3	70%	5	4	80%	5	4	85%	3	4	90%	1	3
Bench Press	40%	10	3	60%	5	3	70%	3	4	80%	3	4	90%	2	4	95%	1	3
DB Bench Press	60%	5	2	70%	5	2	80%	5	2	85%	5	2						
Dips with Weight	60%	5	2	70%	5	2	80%	5	2									
Barbell Curl	60%	5	2	70%	5	2	80%	5	1									
Block Toss		50	2		50	1												
Machine Neck		8	2	70%	8	1												
Ab Crunch		40	1		40	1		40	1									

Day 2

Exercise	Set 1 %	Rp	Rt	Set 2 %	Rp	Rt	Set 3 %	Rp	Rt	Set 4 %	Rp	Rt	Set 5 %	Rp	Rt	Set 6 %	Rp	Rt
Push Press	40%	5	2	60%	3	3	70%	3	3	80%	3	3	85%	3	3			
DB Press	60%	5	3	70%	5	3	80%	5	1									
DB Step-Ups	60%	5	2	70%	5	2	75%	5	2									
DB Lunge	60%	5	2	70%	5	1												
Lat Pulldown	60%	5	2	70%	5	2	80%	5	2									
Low Row	60%	5	2	70%	5	2	80%	5	1									
Barbell Shrug	60%	5	2	70%	5	2	80%	5	1									
Standing Calf	50%	12	2	60%	12	2	70%	12	1									
Partner Neck		10	1															
Finger Walk	6 lb	5	1															
Knee-ups		20	1		20	1		20	1									

Day 3

Exercise	Set 1 %	Rp	Rt	Set 2 %	Rp	Rt	Set 3 %	Rp	Rt	Set 4 %	Rp	Rt	Set 5 %	Rp	Rt	Set 6 %	Rp	Rt
Clean Pull from Knee	40%	5	2	60%	5	3	70%	5	3	80%	3	3	85%	3	3			
Leg Press	40%	10	2	60%	5	4	70%	5	4	80%	3	4	90%	2	2			
Incline Barbell Press	40%	10	3	60%	5	4	70%	5	4	80%	3	4	90%	3	4	95%	1	2
DB Incline	60%	5	3	70%	5	3	80%	5	2									
DB Curl	60%	5	2	70%	5	2	75%	5	1									
Neck Machine		10	2	60%	10	1												
DB Hold	Max Time 1 Set																	
Side Bend		25	1		25	1		25	1									

% = Percentage based on maximum   *Rp*=Rep   *Rt*=Rest

Linemen
3 Day Football Strength ADVANCED

Week 6

Day 1

Exercise	Set 1 %	Rp	Rt	Set 2 %	Rp	Rt	Set 3 %	Rp	Rt	Set 4 %	Rp	Rt	Set 5 %	Rp	Rt	Set 6 %	Rp	Rt
Power Clean	40%	5	3	60%	3	3	70%	3	3	80%	3	3	85%	3	3			
Squat	40%	10	3	60%	5	4	70%	3	4	80%	3	4	90%	2	3			
Bench Press	40%	10	3	60%	5	4	70%	3	4	80%	3	4	90%	3	4	95%	1	3
DB Bench Press	60%	5	2	70%	5	2	80%	3	3	90%	3	2						
Dips with Weight	60%	5	2	70%	5	2	80%	5	2									
Barbell Curl	60%	5	2	70%	5	2	80%	5	1									
Block Toss		50	2		50	1												
Machine Neck		8	2	70%	8	2												
Ab Crunch		50	1		50	1		50	1									

Day 2

Exercise	Set 1 %	Rp	Rt	Set 2 %	Rp	Rt	Set 3 %	Rp	Rt	Set 4 %	Rp	Rt	Set 5 %	Rp	Rt	Set 6 %	Rp	Rt
Push Press	40%	5	3	60%	3	3	70%	3	3	80%	3	3	85%	3	3			
DB Press	60%	5	3	70%	5	3	80%	5	2									
DB Step-Ups	60%	5	3	70%	5	3	80%	5	2									
DB Lunge	60%	5	3	70%	5	1												
Lat Pull-down	60%	5	2	70%	5	2	80%	5	2									
Low Row	60%	5	2	70%	5	2	80%	5	1									
Barbell Shrug	60%	5	2	70%	5	2	80%	5	1									
Standing Calf	50%	12	2	60%	12	2	70%	12	1									
Partner Neck		8	2	70%	8	2	75%	8	1									
Finger Walk	6 lb	6	1															
Knee-ups		25	1		25	1		25	1									

Day 3

Exercise	Set 1 %	Rp	Rt	Set 2 %	Rp	Rt	Set 3 %	Rp	Rt	Set 4 %	Rp	Rt	Set 5 %	Rp	Rt	Set 6 %	Rp	Rt
Clean Pull from Knee	40%	5	2	60%	5	3	70%	5	3	80%	5	3	85%	3	3			
Leg Press	40%	10	2	60%	5	2	70%	5	2	80%	5	2	90%	2	2			
Incline Barbell Press	40%	10	3	60%	5	3	70%	5	3	80%	3	3	85%	3	3	90%	3	3
DB Incline	60%	5	3	70%	5	3	80%	5	2									
DB Curl	60%	5	2	70%	5	2	80%	5	1									
Neck Machine		8	2	70%	8	1												
DB Hold	Max Time 1 Set																	
Side Bend		25	1		25	1		25	1									

% = Percentage based on maximum   Rp=Rep   Rt=Rest

Skill	**Week**
3 Day Football Strength BEGINNER	1

Day 1

Exercise	Set 1 %	Rp	Rt	Set 2 %	Rp	Rt	Set 3 %	Rp	Rt	Set 4 %	Rp	Rt	Set 5 %	Rp	Rt	Set 6 %	Rp	Rt
Clean Pull from Knee	40%	10	2	50%	5	2	55%	5	2									
Squat	40%	10	3	50%	10	3	55%	10	3									
Bench Press	40%	10	3	50%	10	3	55%	10	3									
DB Bench Press	50%	10	3	55%	10	2												
Lat Pull-Down	50%	10	2	55%	10	1												
Barbell Curl	50%	10	2	55%	10	1												
Machine Neck		10	1															
Block Toss		20	1															
Ab Crunch		20	1		20	1												

Day 2

Exercise	Set 1 %	Rp	Rt	Set 2 %	Rp	Rt	Set 3 %	Rp	Rt	Set 4 %	Rp	Rt	Set 5 %	Rp	Rt	Set 6 %	Rp	Rt
DB Military	40%	10	3	50%	10	3	55%	10	3									
DB Step-Ups	50%	10	2	55%	10	1												
Machine Low Row	50%	10	2	55%	10	1												
Barbell Shrug	50%	10	2	55%	10	1												
Reverse Curl	50%	10	2	55%	10	1												
Seated Calf	50%	10	2	55%	10	1												
Finger Walk	6 lb.	1	1															
Knee-ups		10	1		10	1												

Day 3

Exercise	Set 1 %	Rp	Rt	Set 2 %	Rp	Rt	Set 3 %	Rp	Rt	Set 4 %	Rp	Rt	Set 5 %	Rp	Rt	Set 6 %	Rp	Rt
Clean Pull from Knee	40%	5	2	50%	5	3	60%	5	2									
DB Lunge	50%	10	2	55%	10	1												
Incline Barbell Press	40%	10	3	50%	8	3	55%	8	2									
DB Incline	50%	8	2	55%	8	1												
Chin-Ups	Bd Wt	3	2	Bd Wt	3	2												
DB Curl	50%	10	2	55%	10	1												
DB Hold	Max Time 1 Set																	
Partner Neck		10	1															
Side Bend		10	1		10	1												

% = Percentage based on maximum   *Rp*=Rep   *Rt*=Rest

Skill
3 Day Football Strength BEGINNER

Week 2

Day 1

Exercise	Set 1 %	Rp	Rt	Set 2 %	Rp	Rt	Set 3 %	Rp	Rt	Set 4 %	Rp	Rt	Set 5 %	Rp	Rt	Set 6 %	Rp	Rt
Clean Pull from Knee	50%	5	2	55%	5	3	60%	5	3									
Squat	50%	10	3	55%	10	3	60%	10	3									
Bench Press	50%	10	3	55%	10	3	60%	10	3									
DB Bench Press	50%	10	2	55%	10	2	60%	10	2									
Lat Pull-Down	50%	10	2	55%	10	2	60%	10	2									
Barbell Curl	50%	10	2	55%	10	2	60%	10	2									
Machine Neck		10	1															
Block Toss		20	2		20	1												
Ab Crunch		20	1		20	1												

Day 2

Exercise	Set 1 %	Rp	Rt	Set 2 %	Rp	Rt	Set 3 %	Rp	Rt	Set 4 %	Rp	Rt	Set 5 %	Rp	Rt	Set 6 %	Rp	Rt
DB Military	50%	10	3	55%	10	3	60%	10	1									
DB Step-Ups	50%	10	3	55%	10	3	60%	10	1									
Machine Low Row	50%	10	2	55%	10	1												
Barbell Shrug	50%	10	2	55%	10	1												
Reverse Curl	50%	10	2	55%	10	1												
Seated Calf	50%	10	2	55%	10	1												
Finger Walk	6 lb.	1	1															
Knee-ups		10	1		10	1												

Day 3

Exercise	Set 1 %	Rp	Rt	Set 2 %	Rp	Rt	Set 3 %	Rp	Rt	Set 4 %	Rp	Rt	Set 5 %	Rp	Rt	Set 6 %	Rp	Rt
Clean Pull from Knee	50%	5	2	55%	5	3	60%	5	2									
DB Lunge	50%	10	3	55%	10	2												
Incline Barbell Press	50%	10	3	55%	8	3	60%	8	3									
DB Incline	50%	8	3	55%	8	1												
Chin-Ups	Bd Wt	3	2	Bd Wt	3	1												
DB Curl	50%	10	2	55%	10	2	60%	10	1									
DB Hold	Max Time 1 Set																	
Partner Neck		10	1															
Side Bend		10	1		10	1												

% = Percentage based on maximum   *Rp*=Rep   *Rt*=Rest

Skill
3 Day Football Strength BEGINNER

Week 3

Day 1

Exercise	Set 1 %	Rp	Rt	Set 2 %	Rp	Rt	Set 3 %	Rp	Rt	Set 4 %	Rp	Rt	Set 5 %	Rp	Rt	Set 6 %	Rp	Rt
Clean Pull from Knee	50%	5	2	60%	5	3	65%	5	3									
Squat	50%	10	3	60%	10	3	65%	10	3									
Bench Press	50%	10	3	60%	10	3	65%	10	3									
DB Bench Press	50%	10	2	55%	10	2	60%	10	2									
Lat Pull-Down	50%	10	2	55%	10	2	60%	10	2									
Barbell Curl	50%	10	2	55%	10	2	60%	10	2									
Machine Neck		10	2	55%	10	1												
Block Toss		25	2		25	1												
Ab Crunch		25	1		25	1												

Day 2

Exercise	Set 1 %	Rp	Rt	Set 2 %	Rp	Rt	Set 3 %	Rp	Rt	Set 4 %	Rp	Rt	Set 5 %	Rp	Rt	Set 6 %	Rp	Rt
DB Military	50%	10	3	60%	10	3	65%	10	2									
DB Step-Ups	50%	10	3	55%	10	3	60%	10	2									
Machine Low Row	50%	10	2	55%	10	2	60%	10	1									
Barbell Shrug	50%	10	2	55%	10	2	60%	10	1									
Reverse Curl	50%	10	2	55%	10	2	60%	10	1									
Seated Calf	50%	10	2	55%	10	2	60%	10	1									
Finger Walk	6 lb.	2	1															
Knee-ups		12	1		12	1												

Day 3

Exercise	Set 1 %	Rp	Rt	Set 2 %	Rp	Rt	Set 3 %	Rp	Rt	Set 4 %	Rp	Rt	Set 5 %	Rp	Rt	Set 6 %	Rp	Rt
Clean Pull from Knee	50%	5	2	55%	5	2	60%	5	2									
DB Lunge	50%	10	3	60%	10	2												
Incline Barbell Press	50%	10	3	60%	8	3	65%	8	3									
DB Incline	50%	8	3	60%	8	1												
Chin-Ups	Bd Wt	4	2	Bd Wt	4	2												
DB Curl	50%	10	2	55%	10	2	60%	10	1									
DB Hold	Max Time 1 Set																	
Partner Neck		10	1															
Side Bend		12	1		12	1												

% = Percentage based on maximum   *Rp*=Rep   *Rt*=Rest

Skill
3 Day Football Strength BEGINNER

Week
4

Day 1

Exercise	Set 1 %	Rp	Rt	Set 2 %	Rp	Rt	Set 3 %	Rp	Rt	Set 4 %	Rp	Rt	Set 5 %	Rp	Rt	Set 6 %	Rp	Rt
Clean Pull from Knee	50%	5	2	60%	5	3	65%	5	3	70%	5	3						
Squat	50%	10	3	60%	10	3	65%	8	3	70%	6	3						
Bench Press	50%	10	3	60%	10	3	65%	8	3	70%	6	3						
DB Bench Press	55%	8	2	60%	8	2	65%	8	2									
Lat Pull-Down	55%	8	2	60%	8	2	65%	8	2									
Barbell Curl	55%	8	2	60%	8	2	65%	8	2									
Machine Neck		10	2	60%	10	1												
Block Toss		25	2		25	1												
Ab Crunch		30	1		30	1												

Day 2

Exercise	Set 1 %	Rp	Rt	Set 2 %	Rp	Rt	Set 3 %	Rp	Rt	Set 4 %	Rp	Rt	Set 5 %	Rp	Rt	Set 6 %	Rp	Rt
DB Military	50%	10	3	60%	10	3	65%	8	3	70%	6	2						
DB Step-Ups	50%	8	3	60%	8	3	65%	8	1									
Machine Low Row	50%	8	2	60%	8	2	65%	8	1									
Barbell Shrug	50%	8	2	60%	8	2	65%	8	1									
Reverse Curl	50%	8	2	60%	8	2	65%	8	1									
Seated Calf	50%	8	2	60%	8	2	65%	8	1									
Finger Walk	6 lb.	2	1															
Knee-ups		15	1		15	1												

Day 3

Exercise	Set 1 %	Rp	Rt	Set 2 %	Rp	Rt	Set 3 %	Rp	Rt	Set 4 %	Rp	Rt	Set 5 %	Rp	Rt	Set 6 %	Rp	Rt
Clean Pull from Knee	50%	5	2	60%	5	3	70%	5	3									
DB Lunge	50%	8	3	60%	8	3	65%	8	3									
Incline Barbell Press	50%	10	3	60%	8	3	65%	6	3	70%	6	3						
DB Incline	50%	8	3	60%	8	2												
Chin-Ups	Bd Wt	4	3	Bd Wt	4	2												
DB Curl	50%	8	2	60%	8	2	65%	8	1									
DB Hold	Max Time 1 Set																	
Partner Neck		10	1															
Side Bend		15	1		15	1												

% = Percentage based on maximum   *Rp*=Rep   *Rt*=Rest

Skill
3 Day Football Strength BEGINNER

Week 5

Day 1	Set 1			Set 2			Set 3			Set 4			Set 5			Set 6		
Exercise	%	Rp	Rt	%	Rp	Rt	%	Rp	Rt	%	Rp	Rt	%	Rp	Rt	%	Rp	Rt
Clean Pull from Knee	50%	5	2	60%	5	3	65%	5	3	70%	5	3						
Squat	50%	10	3	60%	10	3	65%	8	3	70%	6	3						
Bench Press	50%	10	3	60%	10	3	65%	8	3	70%	6	3						
DB Bench Press	55%	8	2	60%	8	2	65%	8	2									
Lat Pull-Down	55%	8	2	60%	8	2	65%	8	2									
Barbell Curl	55%	8	2	60%	8	2	65%	8	2									
Machine Neck		10	2	60%	10	1												
Block Toss		25	2		25	1												
Ab Crunch		30	1		30	1		30	1									

Day 2	Set 1			Set 2			Set 3			Set 4			Set 5			Set 6		
Exercise	%	Rp	Rt	%	Rp	Rt	%	Rp	Rt	%	Rp	Rt	%	Rp	Rt	%	Rp	Rt
DB Military	50%	10	3	60%	10	3	65%	8	3	70%	6	2						
DB Step-Ups	50%	8	3	60%	8	3	65%	8	1									
Machine Low Row	50%	8	2	60%	8	2	65%	8	1									
Barbell Shrug	50%	8	2	60%	8	2	65%	8	1									
Reverse Curl	50%	8	2	60%	8	2	65%	8	1									
Seated Calf	50%	8	2	60%	8	2	65%	8	1									
Finger Walk	6 lb.	2	1															
Knee-ups		15	1		15	1		15	1									

Day 3	Set 1			Set 2			Set 3			Set 4			Set 5			Set 6		
Exercise	%	Rp	Rt	%	Rp	Rt	%	Rp	Rt	%	Rp	Rt	%	Rp	Rt	%	Rp	Rt
Clean Pull from Knee	50%	5	2	60%	5	3	70%	5	3									
DB Lunge	50%	8	3	60%	8	3	65%	8	3									
Incline Barbell Press	50%	10	3	60%	8	3	65%	6	3	70%	6	3						
DB Incline	50%	8	3	60%	8	2												
Chin-Ups	Bd Wt	4	3	Bd Wt	4	2												
DB Curl	50%	8	2	60%	8	2	65%	8	1									
DB Hold	Max Time 1 Set																	
Partner Neck		10	1															
Side Bend		15	1		15	1												

% = Percentage based on maximum   Rp=Rep   Rt=Rest

Skill
3 Day Football Strength BEGINNER

Week 6

Day 1

Exercise	Set 1 %	Rp	Rt	Set 2 %	Rp	Rt	Set 3 %	Rp	Rt	Set 4 %	Rp	Rt	Set 5 %	Rp	Rt	Set 6 %	Rp	Rt
Clean Pull from Knee	50%	5	3	60%	5	3	70%	5	3	75%	5	3						
Squat	50%	10	3	60%	8	3	72%	6	3	77%	6	3						
Bench Press	50%	10	3	60%	8	3	72%	6	3	77%	6	3						
DB Bench Press	60%	8	2	70%	8	2	75%	8	2									
Lat Pull-Down	60%	8	2	70%	8	2	75%	8	2									
Barbell Curl	50%	8	2	60%	8	2	70%	8	2									
Machine Neck		10	2	60%	10	1												
Block Toss		30	2		30	1												
Ab Crunch		30	1		30	1		30	1									

Day 2

Exercise	Set 1 %	Rp	Rt	Set 2 %	Rp	Rt	Set 3 %	Rp	Rt	Set 4 %	Rp	Rt	Set 5 %	Rp	Rt	Set 6 %	Rp	Rt
DB Military	55%	10	3	60%	8	3	70%	6	3	75%	6	2						
DB Step-Ups	60%	8	3	65%	8	3	70%	8	1									
Machine Low Row	60%	8	2	65%	8	2	70%	8	1									
Barbell Shrug	60%	8	2	65%	8	2	70%	8	1									
Reverse Curl	60%	8	2	65%	8	2	70%	8	1									
Seated Calf	50%	12	2	55%	12	2	60%	12	1									
Finger Walk	6 lb.	4	1															
Knee-ups		15	1		15	1		15	1									

Day 3

Exercise	Set 1 %	Rp	Rt	Set 2 %	Rp	Rt	Set 3 %	Rp	Rt	Set 4 %	Rp	Rt	Set 5 %	Rp	Rt	Set 6 %	Rp	Rt
Clean Pull from Knee	50%	5	2	60%	5	3	70%	5	3	75%	5	3						
DB Lunge	60%	8	3	65%	8	3	70%	8	3									
Incline Barbell Press	50%	10	3	60%	8	3	70%	6	3	75%	6	3						
DB Incline	60%	8	2	70%	8	2	75%	8	2									
Chin-Ups	Bd Wt	5	2	Bd Wt	5	2												
DB Curl	60%	8	2	65%	8	2	70%	8	2									
DB Hold	Max Time 1 Set																	
Partner Neck		10	1															
Side Bend		15	1		15	1		15	1									

% = Percentage based on maximum   Rp=Rep   Rt=Rest

Skill
3 Day Football Strength INTERMEDIATE

Week 1

Day 1	Set 1			Set 2			Set 3			Set 4			Set 5			Set 6		
Exercise	%	Rp	Rt	%	Rp	Rt	%	Rp	Rt	%	Rp	Rt	%	Rp	Rt	%	Rp	Rt
Clean Pull from Knee	40%	5	2	50%	5	2	55%	5	3	60%	5	3						
Squat	40%	10	3	50%	10	3	60%	10	3	75%	3	2						
Bench Press	40%	10	3	50%	10	3	60%	10	3	75%	3	2						
DB Bench	50%	10	3	55%	10	3	60%	10	3									
Dips with Weight	50%	8	3	60%	8	1												
Lat Pull-down	50%	10	2	55%	10	2	60%	10	1									
Barbell Curl	50%	10	2	55%	10	2	60%	10	1									
Block Toss		20	2		20	2												
Neck		10	2	60%	10	1												
Ab Crunch		25	1		25	1												

Day 2	Set 1			Set 2			Set 3			Set 4			Set 5			Set 6		
Exercise	%	Rp	Rt	%	Rp	Rt	%	Rp	Rt	%	Rp	Rt	%	Rp	Rt	%	Rp	Rt
DB Press	50%	10	3	60%	10	3												
DB Step-Ups	50%	10	3	60%	10	2												
DB Lunge	50%	10	3	60%	10	1												
Barbell Shrug	50%	10	2	60%	10	2	65%	10	1									
Standing Calf Raise	50%	10	2	60%	10	1												
Finger Walk	6 lbs.	3	1															
Knee-ups		12	1		12	1												

Day 3	Set 1			Set 2			Set 3			Set 4			Set 5			Set 6		
Exercise	%	Rp	Rt	%	Rp	Rt	%	Rp	Rt	%	Rp	Rt	%	Rp	Rt	%	Rp	Rt
Clean Pull from Knee	40%	5	2	50%	5	3	60%	5	3	65%	5	3						
Leg Press	40%	10	3	50%	10	3	60%	10	1									
Incline Barbell Press	40%	10	3	50%	8	3	60%	8	3	75%	3	3						
DB Incline	50%	8	3	55%	8	3	60%	8	1									
Pull-Ups	Bd Wt	4	2	Bd Wt	4	2												
DB Curl	50%	10	2	55%	10	2	60%	10	1									
Partner Neck		10	1															
DB Hold	Max Time 1 Set																	
Side Bend		15	1		15	1												

% = Percentage based on maximum   Rp=Rep   Rt=Rest

Skill
3 Day Football Strength INTERMEDIATE

Week 2

Day 1

Exercise	%	Rp	Rt	%	Rp	Rt	%	Rp	Rt	%	Rp	Rt	%	Rp	Rt	%	Rp	Rt
	Set 1			Set 2			Set 3			Set 4			Set 5			Set 6		
Clean Pull from Knee	40%	5	2	50%	5	3	60%	5	3	70%	5	3						
Squat	40%	10	3	60%	10	4	70%	10	4	80%	3	3						
Bench Press	40%	10	3	60%	10	4	70%	10	4	80%	3	3						
DB Bench	50%	10	3	60%	10	3	65%	10	3									
Dips with Weight	50%	8	3	60%	8	1												
Lat Pull-down	50%	10	3	60%	10	3	70%	10	1									
Barbell Curl	50%	10	2	60%	10	2	65%	10	1									
Block Toss		20	2		20	2												
Neck		10	2	60%	10	1												
Ab Crunch		30	1		30	1												

Day 2

Exercise	%	Rp	Rt	%	Rp	Rt	%	Rp	Rt	%	Rp	Rt	%	Rp	Rt	%	Rp	Rt
	Set 1			Set 2			Set 3			Set 4			Set 5			Set 6		
DB Press	50%	10	3	60%	10	4	65%	10	2									
DB Step-Ups	50%	10	3	60%	10	2												
DB Lunge	50%	10	3	60%	10	1												
Barbell Shrug	50%	10	2	60%	10	2	70%	10	1									
Standing Calf Raise	50%	10	2	60%	10	2	70%	10	1									
Finger Walk	6 lbs.	3	1															
Knee-ups		12	1		12	1												

Day 3

Exercise	%	Rp	Rt	%	Rp	Rt	%	Rp	Rt	%	Rp	Rt	%	Rp	Rt	%	Rp	Rt
	Set 1			Set 2			Set 3			Set 4			Set 5			Set 6		
Clean Pull from Knee	50%	5	2	60%	5	3	65%	5	3	70%	5	2						
Leg Press	40%	10	3	50%	10	3	60%	10	3	70%	3	2						
Incline Barbell Press	40%	10	3	60%	8	3	70%	8	3	80%	3	3						
DB Incline	50%	8	3	60%	8	3	65%	8	1									
Pull-Ups	Bd Wt	5	2	Bd Wt	5	2												
DB Curl	50%	10	2	60%	10	2	65%	10	1									
Partner Neck		10	2															
DB Hold	Max Time 1 Set																	
Side Bend		15	1		15	1												

% = Percentage based on maximum   *Rp*=Rep   *Rt*=Rest

Skill
3 Day Football Strength INTERMEDIATE

Week 3

Day 1

Exercise	Set 1 %	Rp	Rt	Set 2 %	Rp	Rt	Set 3 %	Rp	Rt	Set 4 %	Rp	Rt	Set 5 %	Rp	Rt	Set 6 %	Rp	Rt
Clean Pull from Knee	40%	5	2	60%	5	3	70%	5	3	75%	5	3						
Squat	40%	10	3	60%	5	3	70%	3	3	80%	3	3						
Bench Press	40%	10	3	60%	5	3	70%	5	3	75%	5	3	80%	3	3			
DB Bench	60%	8	3	65%	8	3	70%	8	2									
Dips with Weight	60%	8	3	70%	8	1												
Lat Pull-down	60%	8	3	70%	8	3	75%	8	1									
Barbell Curl	60%	10	2	65%	10	3	70%	10	1									
Block Toss		20	2		20	1												
Neck		10	2	60%	10	1												
Ab Crunch		30	1		30	1												

Day 2

Exercise	Set 1 %	Rp	Rt	Set 2 %	Rp	Rt	Set 3 %	Rp	Rt	Set 4 %	Rp	Rt	Set 5 %	Rp	Rt	Set 6 %	Rp	Rt
DB Press	50%	8	3	60%	8	3	70%	8	3									
DB Step-Ups	50%	8	3	60%	8	3	70%	8	2									
DB Lunge	50%	8	3	60%	8	3												
Barbell Shrug	60%	8	2	70%	8	2	75%	8	1									
Standing Calf Raise	50%	10	2	60%	10	2	70%	10	1									
Finger Walk	6 lbs.	4	1															
Knee-ups		15	1		15	1												

Day 3

Exercise	Set 1 %	Rp	Rt	Set 2 %	Rp	Rt	Set 3 %	Rp	Rt	Set 4 %	Rp	Rt	Set 5 %	Rp	Rt	Set 6 %	Rp	Rt
Clean Pull from Knee	50%	5	2	60%	5	3	70%	5	3									
Leg Press	40%	10	3	50%	5	3	60%	5	3	70%	5	2						
Incline Barbell Press	40%	10	3	60%	5	3	70%	5	3	80%	3	3						
DB Incline	60%	8	3	65%	8	3	70%	8	1									
Pull-Ups	Bd Wt	6	2	Bd Wt	6	1												
DB Curl	60%	10	2	65%	10	3	70%	10	1									
Partner Neck		10	1															
DB Hold	Max Time 1 Set																	
Side Bend		20	1		20	1												

% = Percentage based on maximum   *Rp*=Rep   *Rt*=Rest

Skill
3 Day Football Strength INTERMEDIATE

Week 4

Day 1

Exercise	Set 1 %	Rp	Rt	Set 2 %	Rp	Rt	Set 3 %	Rp	Rt	Set 4 %	Rp	Rt	Set 5 %	Rp	Rt	Set 6 %	Rp	Rt
Clean Pull from Knee	40%	5	2	60%	5	3	70%	5	3	80%	3	3						
Squat	40%	10	3	60%	5	3	70%	5	3	80%	5	3	85%	2	2			
Bench Press	40%	10	3	60%	5	3	70%	5	3	80%	5	3	85%	3	3			
DB Bench	60%	8	3	65%	8	3	70%	8	3									
Dips with Weight	60%	8	3	65%	8	3	70%	8	1									
Lat Pull-down	60%	8	2	70%	8	2	75%	8	1									
Barbell Curl	60%	8	2	70%	8	2	75%	8	1									
Block Toss		20	2		20	1												
Neck		8	2	65%	8	1												
Ab Crunch		30	1		30	1		30	1									

Day 2

Exercise	Set 1	R	Set 2	R	Set 3	R	Set 4	R	Set 5	R	Set 6	R
DB Press	60% 8	3	70% 8	3	75% 8	2						
DB Step-Ups	50% 8	3	60% 8	3	70% 8	3						
DB Lunge	50% 8	3	60% 8	3	70% 8	3						
Barbell Shrug	60% 8	2	70% 8	2	75% 8	1						
Standing Calf Raise	50% 12	2	60% 12	2	70% 12	1						
Finger Walk	6 lbs. 4	1										
Knee-ups	15	1	15	1	15	1						

Day 3

Exercise	Set 1	R	Set 2	R	Set 3	R	Set 4	R	Set 5	R	Set 6	R
Clean Pull from Knee	50% 5	2	60% 5	3	70% 5	3	80% 5	3				
Leg Press	40% 10	2	50% 5	2	60% 5	3	70% 5	2	80% 3	2		
Incline Barbell Press	40% 10	3	60% 5	3	70% 5	3	80% 5	3				
DB Incline	60% 8	3	65% 8	3	70% 8	2						
Pull-Ups	Bd Wt 7	2	Bd Wt 7	1								
DB Curl	60% 8	2	70% 8	2	75% 8	1						
Partner Neck	10	2										
DB Hold	Max Time 1 Set											
Side Bend	20	1	20	1	20	1						

% = Percentage based on maximum   Rp=Rep   Rt=Rest

Skill
3 Day Football Strength INTERMEDIATE

Week 5

Day 1

Exercise	Set 1			Set 2			Set 3			Set 4			Set 5			Set 6		
	%	Rp	Rt	%	Rp	Rt	%	Rp	Rt	%	Rp	Rt	%	Rp	Rt	%	Rp	Rt
Clean Pull from Knee	50%	5	3	60%	5	3	70%	5	3	80%	5	3						
Squat	40%	10	3	60%	5	3	70%	5	3	80%	3	3	90%	1	3			
Bench Press	40%	10	3	60%	5	3	70%	5	3	80%	5	3	85%	5	3			
DB Bench	60%	6	3	70%	6	3	75%	6	3									
Dips with Weight	60%	6	3	70%	6	3	75%	6	1									
Lat Pull-down	60%	6	2	70%	6	2	75%	6	2	80%	6	1						
Barbell Curl	60%	8	2	70%	8	2	75%	8	1									
Block Toss		20	2		20	1												
Neck		8	2	70%	8	2												
Ab Crunch		30	1		30	1		30	1									

Day 2

Exercise	Set 1			Set 2			Set 3			Set 4			Set 5			Set 6		
	%	Rp	Rt	%	Rp	Rt	%	Rp	Rt	%	Rp	Rt	%	Rp	Rt	%	Rp	Rt
DB Press	60%	6	3	70%	6	3	80%	6	3									
DB Step-Ups	60%	6	2	70%	6	2	75%	6	2									
DB Lunge	60%	6	2	70%	6	2	75%	6	1									
Barbell Shrug	60%	6	2	70%	6	2	75%	6	1									
Standing Calf Raise	60%	12	2	65%	12	2	70%	12	1									
Finger Walk	6 lbs.	4	1															
Knee-ups		15	1		15	1		15	1									

Day 3

Exercise	Set 1			Set 2			Set 3			Set 4			Set 5			Set 6		
	%	Rp	Rt	%	Rp	Rt	%	Rp	Rt	%	Rp	Rt	%	Rp	Rt	%	Rp	Rt
Clean Pull from Knee	50%	5	2	60%	3	3	70%	3	3	80%	3	3						
Leg Press	40%	10	2	60%	5	2	70%	5	2	80%	5	2	85%	2	2			
Incline Barbell Press	40%	10	3	60%	5	3	70%	5	3	80%	3	3	85%	3	3			
DB Incline	60%	6	3	70%	6	3	75%	6	1									
Pull-Ups	Bd Wt	8	3	Bd Wt	8	1												
DB Curl	60%	8	2	70%	8	2	75%	8	1									
Partner Neck		10	2															
DB Hold	Max Time 1 Set																	
Side Bend		20	1		20	1		20	1									

% = Percentage based on maximum   *Rp*=Rep   *Rt*=Rest

Skill
3 Day Football Strength INTERMEDIATE

Week
6

Day 1

Exercise	Set 1 %	Rp	Rt	Set 2 %	Rp	Rt	Set 3 %	Rp	Rt	Set 4 %	Rp	Rt	Set 5 %	Rp	Rt	Set 6 %	Rp	Rt
Clean Pull from Knee	40%	5	3	60%	3	3	70%	3	4	80%	3	4	85%	3	3			
Squat	40%	10	3	60%	5	3	70%	5	4	80%	3	4	85%	3	4	90%	1	3
Bench Press	40%	10	3	60%	5	3	70%	5	3	80%	3	3	85%	3	3	90%	1	3
DB Bench	60%	6	3	70%	6	3	80%	6	3									
Dips with Weight	60%	6	3	70%	6	3	80%	6	1									
Lat Pull-down	60%	6	2	70%	6	2	80%	6	1									
Barbell Curl	60%	8	2	70%	8	2	75%	8	1									
Block Toss		20	2		20	1												
Neck		8	2	70%	8	2	75%	8	1									
Ab Crunch		35	1		35	1		35	1									

Day 2

Exercise	Set 1 %	Rp	Rt	Set 2 %	Rp	Rt	Set 3 %	Rp	Rt	Set 4 %	Rp	Rt	Set 5 %	Rp	Rt	Set 6 %	Rp	Rt
DB Press	60%	6	3	70%	6	3	80%	6	3									
DB Step-Ups	60%	6	3	70%	6	3	75%	6	3									
DB Lunge	60%	6	3	70%	6	3	75%	6	3									
Barbell Shrug	60%	6	2	70%	6	2	75%	6	2									
Standing Calf Raise	60%	12	2	70%	12	2	75%	12	1									
Finger Walk	6 lbs.	5	1															
Knee-ups		20	1		20	1		20	1									

Day 3

Exercise	Set 1 %	Rp	Rt	Set 2 %	Rp	Rt	Set 3 %	Rp	Rt	Set 4 %	Rp	Rt	Set 5 %	Rp	Rt	Set 6 %	Rp	Rt
Clean Pull from Knee	50%	5	2	60%	3	3	70%	3	3	80%	3	3						
Leg Press	40%	10	2	60%	5	2	70%	5	2	80%	5	2	90%	2	3			
Incline Barbell Press	40%	10	3	60%	5	3	70%	5	3	80%	3	3	85%	3	3	90%	1	3
DB Incline	60%	6	3	70%	6	3	80%	6	3									
Pull-Ups	Bd Wt	10	3	Bd Wt	8	1												
DB Curl	60%	8	2	70%	8	2	75%	8	2									
Partner Neck		8	2															
DB Hold	Max Time 1 Set																	
Side Bend		25	1		25	1		25	1									

% = Percentage based on maximum   *Rp*=Rep   *Rt*=Rest

Skill
3 Day Football Strength ADVANCED

Week 1

Day 1

Exercise	Set 1 %	Rp	Rt	Set 2 %	Rp	Rt	Set 3 %	Rp	Rt	Set 4 %	Rp	Rt	Set 5 %	Rp	Rt	Set 6 %	Rp	Rt
Clean Pull from Knee	40%	5	2	60%	5	2	65%	5	3									
Squat	40%	10	4	60%	10	4	65%	10	4	75%	3	4	85%	1	2			
Bench Press	40%	10	4	60%	10	4	65%	10	4	70%	10	4	80%	3	2	90%	1	3
DB Bench	60%	10	3	70%	10	3												
Dips with Weight	50%	8	3	60%	8	2												
Barbell Curl	50%	10	2	60%	10	2	65%	10	1									
Block Toss		20	2		20	1												
Neck		10	1															
Ab Crunch		30	1															

Day 1

Exercise	Set 1 %	Rp	Rt	Set 2 %	Rp	Rt	Set 3 %	Rp	Rt	Set 4 %	Rp	Rt	Set 5 %	Rp	Rt	Set 6 %	Rp	Rt
DB Press	50%	8	3	60%	8	3	65%	8	2									
DB Step-Up	50%	10	3	55%	10	2												
DB Lunge	50%	10	3	55%	10	2												
Chin-Ups	Bd Wt	5	3	Bd Wt	5	2												
Barbell Shrug	50%	10	2	55%	10	2	60%	10	1									
Standing Calf Raise	50%	10	2	55%	10	1												
Partner Neck		10	1															
Finger Walk	6 lbs	3	1															
Knee-ups		15	1		15	1												

Day 3

Exercise	Set 1 %	Rp	Rt	Set 2 %	Rp	Rt	Set 3 %	Rp	Rt	Set 4 %	Rp	Rt	Set 5 %	Rp	Rt	Set 6 %	Rp	Rt
Clean Pull from Knee	50%	3	2	60%	3	3	70%	3	3	75%	3	2						
Leg Press	40%	10	4	50%	10	4	60%	10	4	75%	3	2						
Incline Barbell Press	40%	10	4	60%	8	4	65%	8	4	75%	3	3						
DB Incline	50%	8	3	60%	8	2												
Bicep Curl	40%	10	2	50%	10	2	60%	10	1									
DB Hold	Max Time 1 Set																	
Side Bend		20	1		20	1												

% = Percentage based on maximum   *Rp*=Rep   *Rt*=Rest

Skill
3 Day Football Strength ADVANCED

Week 2

Day 1

Exercise	Set 1 %	Rp	Rt	Set 2 %	Rp	Rt	Set 3 %	Rp	Rt	Set 4 %	Rp	Rt	Set 5 %	Rp	Rt	Set 6 %	Rp	Rt
Clean Pull from Knee	40%	5	2	60%	5	3	65%	5	3	70%	5	2						
Squat	40%	10	4	60%	8	4	70%	8	4	80%	3	2	90%	1	2			
Bench Press	40%	10	4	60%	8	4	70%	8	4	75%	8	4	85%	3	4	90%	1	3
DB Bench	60%	8	3	70%	8	3	75%	8	3									
Dips with Weight	60%	8	3	70%	8	2												
Barbell Curl	50%	10	2	60%	10	3	70%	10	1									
Block Toss		25	2		25	1												
Neck		10	2	60%	10	1												
Ab Crunch		30	1		30	1												

Day 2

Exercise	Set 1 %	Rp	Rt	Set 2 %	Rp	Rt	Set 3 %	Rp	Rt	Set 4 %	Rp	Rt	Set 5 %	Rp	Rt	Set 6 %	Rp	Rt
DB Press	50%	8	2	60%	8	3	70%	8	2									
DB Step-Up	50%	8	3	55%	8	3	60%	8	2									
DB Lunge	50%	8	3	60%	8	3												
Chin-ups	Bd Wt	6	3	Bd Wt	6	2												
Barbell Shrug	50%	10	2	60%	10	2	70%	10	1									
Standing Calf Raise	50%	10	2	60%	10	1												
Partner Neck		10	1															
Finger Walk	6 lbs	3	2															
Knee-ups		15	1		15	1												

Day 3

Exercise	Set 1 %	Rp	Rt	Set 2 %	Rp	Rt	Set 3 %	Rp	Rt	Set 4 %	Rp	Rt	Set 5 %	Rp	Rt	Set 6 %	Rp	Rt
Clean Pull from Knee	50%	5	2	60%	3	3	70%	3	3	75%	3	2						
Leg Press	40%	10	4	60%	8	4	70%	8	4	80%	3	2						
Incline Barbell Press	40%	10	4	60%	8	4	70%	8	4	80%	3	2						
DB Incline	60%	8	3	65%	8	2												
Bicep Curl	50%	10	2	60%	10	2	65%	10	3									
DB Hold	Max Time 1 Set																	
Side Bend		20	1		20	1												

% = Percentage based on maximum   *Rp*=Rep   *Rt*=Rest

Skill
3 Day Football Strength ADVANCED

Week 3

Day 1	Set 1			Set 2			Set 3			Set 4			Set 5			Set 6		
Exercise	%	Rp	Rt	%	Rp	Rt	%	Rp	Rt	%	Rp	Rt	%	Rp	Rt	%	Rp	Rt
Clean Pull from Knee	40%	5	2	60%	5	3	70%	5	3	75%	5	3						
Squat	40%	10	4	60%	6	4	70%	6	4	75%	6	4	85%	2	4	90%	1	2
Bench Press	50%	10	4	70%	6	4	75%	6	4	80%	6	4	90%	2	4	95%	1	3
DB Bench	60%	6	3	70%	6	3	80%	6	3									
Dips with Weight	60%	6	3	70%	6	3	75%	6	1									
Barbell Curl	60%	8	2	70%	8	3	75%	8	1									
Block Toss		30	2		30	1												
Neck		10	2	60%	10	1												
Ab Crunch		30	1		30	1		30	1									

Day 1	Set 1			Set 2			Set 3			Set 4			Set 5			Set 6		
Exercise	%	Rp	Rt	%	Rp	Rt	%	Rp	Rt	%	Rp	Rt	%	Rp	Rt	%	Rp	Rt
DB Press	50%	6	3	60%	6	3	70%	6	3	75%	6							
DB Step-Up	50%	5	3	60%	5	3	70%	5	2									
DB Lunge	50%	5	3	60%	5	3	70%	5	2									
Chin-Ups	Bd Wt	7	3	Bd Wt	7	2												
Barbell Shrug	60%	8	2	70%	8	2	75%	8	2									
Standing Calf Raise	50%	12	2	60%	12	2	65%	12	2									
Partner Neck		10	1															
Finger Walk	6 lbs	4	1															
Knee-ups		15	1		15	1		15	1									

Day 3	Set 1			Set 2			Set 3			Set 4			Set 5			Set 6		
Exercise	%	Rp	Rt	%	Rp	Rt	%	Rp	Rt	%	Rp	Rt	%	Rp	Rt	%	Rp	Rt
Clean Pull from Knee	40%	5	2	60%	3	3	70%	3	3	80%	3	3						
Leg Press	40%	10	3	60%	6	4	70%	6	4	75%	6	4	85%	2	2			
Incline Barbell Press	40%	10	4	60%	6	4	70%	6	4	75%	6	4	85%	2	3			
DB Incline	60%	8	3	70%	6	3												
Bicep Curl	60%	8	2	65%	8	3	70%	8	2									
DB Hold	Max Time 1 Set																	
Side Bend		20	1		20	1		20	1									

% = Percentage based on maximum   *Rp*=Rep   *Rt*=Rest

Skill
3 Day Football Strength ADVANCED

Week 4

Day 1

Exercise	Set 1 %	Rp	Rt	Set 2 %	Rp	Rt	Set 3 %	Rp	Rt	Set 4 %	Rp	Rt	Set 5 %	Rp	Rt	Set 6 %	Rp	Rt
Clean Pull from Knee	40%	5	3	60%	5	4	70%	5	4	75%	5	4	80%	3	4			
Squat	40%	10	4	60%	5	4	70%	5	4	80%	5	4	90%	2	3			
Bench Press	40%	10	4	60%	5	4	70%	5	4	80%	5	4	85%	5	3	90%	2	3
DB Bench	60%	5	3	70%	5	3	80%	5	3									
Dips with Weight	60%	6	3	70%	6	3	80%	6	1									
Barbell Curl	60%	8	2	70%	8	2	75%	8	1									
Block Toss		35	2		35	1												
Neck		8	2	60%	8	1												
Ab Crunch		35	1		35	1		35	1									

Day 2

Exercise	Set 1 %	Rp	Rt	Set 2 %	Rp	Rt	Set 3 %	Rp	Rt	Set 4 %	Rp	Rt	Set 5 %	Rp	Rt	Set 6 %	Rp	Rt
DB Press	60%	6	3	65%	6	3	70%	6	3	75%	6	1						
DB Step-Up	50%	5	3	60%	5	3	70%	5	3									
DB Lunge	50%	5	3	60%	5	3	70%	5	3									
Chin-Ups	Bd Wt	8	3	Bd Wt	8	2												
Barbell Shrug	60%	8	2	65%	8	2	75%	8	2									
Standing Calf Raise	50%	12	2	60%	12	2	65%	12	2									
Partner Neck		10	1															
Finger Walk	6 lbs	3	2	6 lbs	2	2												
Knee-ups		20	1		20	1		20	1									

Day 3

Exercise	Set 1 %	Rp	Rt	Set 2 %	Rp	Rt	Set 3 %	Rp	Rt	Set 4 %	Rp	Rt	Set 5 %	Rp	Rt	Set 6 %	Rp	Rt
Clean Pull from Knee	40%	5	2	60%	3	3	70%	3	3	80%	3	3	85%	3	3			
Leg Press	40%	10	2	60%	5	4	70%	5	4	80%	5	4	90%	2	2			
Incline Barbell Press	40%	10	4	60%	5	4	70%	5	4	80%	5	4	90%	2	3			
DB Incline	60%	5	3	70%	5	3	75%	5	2									
Bicep Curl	60%	8	2	65%	8	2	70%	8	1									
DB Hold	Max Time 1 Set																	
Side Bend		25	1		25	1		25	1									

% = Percentage based on maximum   *Rp*=Rep   *Rt*=Rest

Skill
3 Day Football Strength ADVANCED

Week 5

Day 1

Exercise	Set 1 %	Rp	Rt	Set 2 %	Rp	Rt	Set 3 %	Rp	Rt	Set 4 %	Rp	Rt	Set 5 %	Rp	Rt	Set 6 %	Rp	Rt
Clean Pull from Knee	50%	5	3	60%	5	3	70%	5	3	80%	5	3						
Squat	40%	10	4	60%	5	4	70%	5	4	80%	3	4	85%	3	4	90%	1	3
Bench Press	40%	10	4	60%	5	4	70%	3	4	80%	3	4	90%	3	4	95%	1	3
DB Bench	60%	5	3	70%	5	3	80%	5	3									
Dips with Weight	60%	5	3	70%	5	3	80%	5	1									
Barbell Curl	60%	5	2	70%	5	2	80%	5	1									
Block Toss		40	2		40	1												
Neck		8	2	70%	8	1												
Ab Crunch		40	1		40	1		40	1									

Day 1

Exercise	Set 1 %	Rp	Rt	Set 2 %	Rp	Rt	Set 3 %	Rp	Rt	Set 4 %	Rp	Rt	Set 5 %	Rp	Rt	Set 6 %	Rp	Rt
DB Press	60%	5	3	70%	5	3	75%	5	3	80%	5	2						
DB Step-Up	60%	5	3	70%	5	3	75%	5	2									
DB Lunge	60%	5	3	70%	5	3	75%	5	2									
Chin-Ups	Bd Wt	10	3	Bd Wt	8	2												
Barbell Shrug	60%	5	2	70%	5	2	80%	5	1									
Standing Calf Raise	50%	12	2	60%	12	2	70%	12	1									
Partner Neck		10	1															
Finger Walk	6 lbs	3	2	6 lbs	3	2												
Knee-ups		20	1		20	1		20	1									

Day 3

Exercise	Set 1 %	Rp	Rt	Set 2 %	Rp	Rt	Set 3 %	Rp	Rt	Set 4 %	Rp	Rt	Set 5 %	Rp	Rt	Set 6 %	Rp	Rt
Clean Pull from Knee	40%	5	2	60%	3	3	70%	3	3	80%	3	3	85%	3	3			
Leg Press	40%	10	3	60%	5	3	70%	5	3	80%	5	3	90%	2	2			
Incline Barbell Press	40%	10	4	60%	5	4	70%	3	4	80%	3	4	85%	3	3			
DB Incline	60%	5	3	70%	5	3	80%	5	2									
Bicep Curl	60%	5	2	70%	5	2	75%	5	1									
DB Hold	Max Time 1 Set																	
Side Bend		25	1		25	1		25	1									

% = Percentage based on maximum   *Rp*=Rep   *Rt*=Rest

Skill
3 Day Football Strength ADVANCED

Week 6

Day 1

Exercise	Set 1 %	Rp	Rt	Set 2 %	Rp	Rt	Set 3 %	Rp	Rt	Set 4 %	Rp	Rt	Set 5 %	Rp	Rt	Set 6 %	Rp	Rt
Clean Pull from Knee	40%	5	3	60%	3	4	70%	3	4	80%	3	4	85%	3	4	90%	1	2
Squat	40%	10	4	60%	5	4	70%	3	4	80%	3	4	90%	1	3			
Bench Press	40%	10	4	60%	5	4	70%	3	4	80%	3	4	85%	3	4	90%	3	3
DB Bench	60%	5	3	70%	5	3	80%	5	3									
Dips with Weight	60%	5	3	70%	5	3	80%	5	1									
Barbell Curl	60%	5	2	70%	5	2	80%	5	1									
Block Toss		50	2		50	1												
Neck		8	2	70%	8	1												
Ab Crunch		50	1		50	1		50	1									

Day 2

Exercise	Set 1 %	Rp	Rt	Set 2 %	Rp	Rt	Set 3 %	Rp	Rt	Set 4 %	Rp	Rt	Set 5 %	Rp	Rt	Set 6 %	Rp	Rt
DB Press	60%	5	3	70%	5	3	75%	5	3	80%	5	2						
DB Step-Up	60%	5	3	70%	5	3	75%	5	3									
DB Lunge	60%	5	3	70%	5	3	75%	5	3									
Chin-Ups	Bd Wt	10	4	Bd Wt	10	2												
Barbell Shrug	60%	5	2	70%	5	2	80%	5	1									
Standing Calf Raise	50%	12	2	60%	12	2	70%	12	1									
Partner Neck		10	1															
Finger Walk	6 lbs	6	2															
Knee-ups		25	1		25	1		25	1									

Day 3

Exercise	Set 1 %	Rp	Rt	Set 2 %	Rp	Rt	Set 3 %	Rp	Rt	Set 4 %	Rp	Rt	Set 5 %	Rp	Rt	Set 6 %	Rp	Rt
Clean Pull from Knee	40%	5	2	60%	3	3	70%	3	3	80%	3	3	85%	3	3			
Leg Press	40%	10	3	60%	5	3	70%	5	3	80%	5	3	90%	2	2			
Incline Barbell Press	40%	10	3	60%	5	3	70%	3	3	80%	3	3	85%	3	3	90%	1	3
DB Incline	60%	5	3	70%	5	3	80%	5	3									
Bicep Curl	60%	5	2	70%	5	2	75%	5	2									
DB Hold	Max Time 1 Set																	
Side Bend		25	1		25	1		25	1									

% = Percentage based on maximum   Rp=Rep   Rt=Rest

How to Get in Football Shape

STRENGTH TRAINING

Percentage Guide

Estimated Maximum (in Pounds)

Percentages

	10	20	30	40	50	60	70	80	90	100	110	120	130	140	150	160	170	180	190	200	210	220	230	240	250	260	270	280	290
30%	3	6	9	12	15	18	21	24	27	30	33	36	39	42	45	48	51	54	57	60	63	66	69	72	75	78	81	84	87
35%	4	7	11	14	18	21	25	28	32	35	39	42	46	49	53	56	60	63	67	70	74	77	81	84	88	91	95	98	102
40%	4	8	12	16	20	24	28	32	36	40	44	48	52	56	60	64	68	72	76	80	84	88	92	96	100	104	108	112	116
45%	5	9	14	18	23	27	32	36	41	45	50	54	59	63	68	72	77	81	86	90	95	99	104	108	113	117	122	126	131
50%	5	10	15	20	25	30	35	40	45	50	55	60	65	70	75	80	85	90	95	100	105	110	115	120	125	130	135	140	145
55%	6	11	17	22	28	33	39	44	50	55	61	66	72	77	83	88	94	99	105	110	116	121	127	132	138	143	149	154	160
60%	6	12	18	24	30	36	42	48	54	60	66	72	78	84	90	96	102	108	114	120	126	132	138	144	150	156	162	168	174
65%	7	13	20	26	33	39	46	52	59	65	72	78	85	91	98	104	111	117	124	130	137	143	150	156	163	169	176	182	189
70%	7	14	21	28	35	42	49	56	63	70	77	84	91	98	105	112	119	126	133	140	147	154	161	168	175	182	189	196	203
75%	8	15	23	30	38	45	53	60	68	75	83	90	98	105	113	120	128	135	143	150	158	165	173	180	188	195	203	210	218
80%	8	16	24	32	40	48	56	64	72	80	88	96	104	112	120	128	136	144	152	160	168	176	184	192	200	208	216	224	232
85%	9	17	26	34	43	51	60	68	77	85	94	102	111	119	128	136	145	153	162	170	179	187	196	204	213	221	230	238	247
90%	9	18	27	36	45	54	63	72	81	90	99	108	117	126	135	144	153	162	171	180	189	198	207	216	225	234	243	252	261
95%	10	19	29	38	48	57	67	76	86	95	105	114	124	133	143	152	162	171	181	190	200	209	219	228	238	247	257	266	276
100%	10	20	30	40	50	60	70	80	90	100	110	120	130	140	150	160	170	180	190	200	210	220	230	240	250	260	270	280	290
105%	11	21	32	42	53	63	74	84	95	105	116	126	137	147	158	168	179	189	200	210	221	231	242	252	263	273	284	294	305

Estimated Maximum: the maximum amount of weight with which you can manage 1 rep of the exercise in question.

Estimated Maximum

300	310	320	330	340	350	360	370	380	390	400	410	420	430	440	450	460	470	480	490	500	510	520	530	540	550	560	570	580	590	600
90	93	96	99	102	105	108	111	114	117	120	123	126	129	132	135	138	141	144	147	150	153	156	159	162	165	168	171	174	177	180
105	109	112	116	119	123	126	130	133	137	140	144	147	151	154	158	161	165	168	172	175	179	182	186	189	193	196	200	203	207	210
120	124	128	132	136	140	144	148	152	156	160	164	168	172	176	180	184	188	192	196	200	204	208	212	216	220	224	228	232	236	240
135	140	144	149	153	158	162	167	171	176	180	185	189	194	198	203	207	212	216	221	225	230	234	239	243	248	252	257	261	266	270
150	155	160	165	170	175	180	185	190	195	200	205	210	215	220	225	230	235	240	245	250	255	260	265	270	275	280	285	290	295	300
165	171	176	182	187	193	198	204	209	215	220	226	231	237	242	248	253	259	264	270	275	281	286	292	297	303	308	314	319	325	330
180	186	192	198	204	210	216	222	228	234	240	246	252	258	264	270	276	282	288	294	300	306	312	318	324	330	336	342	348	354	360
195	202	208	215	221	228	234	241	247	254	260	267	273	280	286	293	299	306	312	319	325	332	338	345	351	358	364	371	377	384	390
210	217	224	231	238	245	252	259	266	273	280	287	294	301	308	315	322	329	336	343	350	357	364	371	378	385	392	399	406	413	420
225	233	240	248	255	263	270	278	285	293	300	308	315	323	330	338	345	353	360	368	375	383	390	398	405	413	420	428	435	443	450
240	248	256	264	272	280	288	296	304	312	320	328	336	344	352	360	368	376	384	392	400	408	416	424	432	440	448	456	464	472	480
255	264	272	281	289	298	306	315	323	332	340	349	357	366	374	383	391	400	408	417	425	434	442	451	459	468	476	485	493	502	510
270	279	288	297	306	315	324	333	342	351	360	369	378	387	396	405	414	423	432	441	450	459	468	477	486	495	504	513	522	531	540
285	295	304	314	323	333	342	352	361	371	380	390	399	409	418	428	437	447	456	466	475	485	494	504	513	523	532	542	551	561	570
300	310	320	330	340	350	360	370	380	390	400	410	420	430	440	450	460	470	480	490	500	510	520	530	540	550	560	570	580	590	600
315	326	336	347	357	368	378	389	399	410	420	431	441	452	462	473	483	494	504	515	525	536	546	557	567	578	588	599	609	620	630

Strength Training Journal

Date	Exercise	Weight	Repetitions	Rest Time

Strength Training Journal

Date	Exercise	Weight	Repetitions	Rest Time

Strength Training Journal

Date	Exercise	Weight	Repetitions	Rest Time

Strength Training Journal

Date	Exercise	Weight	Repetitions	Rest Time

Strength Training Journal

Date	Exercise	Weight	Repetitions	Rest Time

Strength Training Journal

Date	Exercise	Weight	Repetitions	Rest Time

DVD Index

Track Name	Track Number
Low Bar Squat	3
High Bar Squat	4
Leg Press	5
Clean Pull from the Knee	6
Dumbbell Step-up	7
Dumbbell Lunge	8
Intro to Abdominals	9
Hanging Knee-ups	10
Ab Circuit	11
Bert Hill Tips	12
Bench Press	13
Incline Barbell Press	14
Hammer Iso Low Row	15
Lat Pull-down	16
Breathing	17
Barbell Military Press	18
Dumbbell Incline	19
Dumbbell Bench	20
How Much Weight?	21
Barbell Curl	22
Dumbbell Press	23
Bicep Curls	24
Adding Weight	25
Barbell Shrug	26
Neck Exercises	27
Hand Exercises	28
Block Toss	29
Finger Walk	30
Fat Bar Curl	31
Dumbbell Hold	32
Closing Comments	33

About Bert Hill

Bert Hill spent eleven seasons overseeing the Detroit Lions' strength and conditioning program. In addition to this role, Hill spent time assisting with the Lions' offensive line.

Hill originally came to the Lions in March 1990 following his second stint at Texas A&M as strength and conditioning coach. While in College Station, the Aggies won three consecutive Southwest Conference titles between 1985-87.

Hill played linebacker at Marion Military Institute Jr. College in Alabama during 1976-77, and one season at Wichita State in 1978. He earned his bachelor's degree in physical education from Auburn University at Montgomery in 1980. In 1982, he received his master's degree at Auburn in physical education, with an emphasis in strength physiology.